Michael Viola

25 YEARS OF PHILADELPHIA REGIONAL HISTORY

Click!

Life Through The Lens Of A News Photographer

By Michael Viola

Staff Photographer

The Philadelphia Inquirer

COVER DESIGN: Louis L. Chap

COVER PHOTOGRAPHY: H. Donald Kroitzsh

FOREWORD: Edgar Williams

TEXT AND CAPTIONS: Michael Viola & The Philadelphia Inquirer

PHOTOGRAPHY: Michael Viola

PUBLISHER & EDITOR: H. Donald Kroitzsh

DESIGNER: Louis L. Chap

ASSISTANT EDITORS: Anne C. Pace-Rosa

                       Kim Cheswick

                       Barbara A. Ritchotte

Printed and bound in the United States of America

Published by:
Five Corners Publications, Ltd.
P O Box 66
Bridgewater, Vermont 05034
USA

Click! Life Through The Lens Of A News Photographer
ISBN: 1-886699-09-7

ACKNOWLEDGEMENTS

The photographs in this book are some personal favorites from my life "on the street" as a staff photographer for *The Philadelphia Inquirer*.

For nearly 25 years, I lived in the best of two worlds—a job with a nice salary and good benefits, and a seat ringside wherever I was sent, accumulating enough experiences to enrich a dozen lifetimes.

The newspaper sends you there, but what you bring back depends on your own special skills, imagination, talent and enthusiasm. A half dozen photographers may scramble shoulder-to-shoulder for a picture, but it is possible for just one of them, shooting "smarter," to come away with *the* defining photo that best represents that event.

A photographer's workweek is predictable, but his work is not. Nice clothes? You'll go to a fire. Dress casually, and you may end up at the opera. News photographers anticipate each day with a sense of excitement, because it will bring new surprises and challenges; no new day is like any of the old ones.

Photographers don't do it alone. They have photo editors, and managing editors, and executive editors, who direct and cajole and plead and urge them on. I am lucky to have worked with some of the very best.

Gene Roberts turned *The Inquirer* into a great newspaper. He is a champion of photographic journalism and is as enthused about pictures as he is about words. He challenged us all—photographers and reporters alike—to get and tell the story, and "let the reader see." He made sure we got the time and resources we needed to do it right.

This book would not exist without the time, advice, encouragement and support of *The Inquirer's* current senior editors, Maxwell King, editor, and Gene Foreman, deputy editor, to whom I'm most grateful.

I would also like to express my appreciation to Frank Glacklin, lab chief, and Richard Titley for their assistance in the final processing of many of these pictures.

I am indebted to *The Inquirer's* fine reporting staff, whose stories led to many of these photographs, and in particular to Edgar Williams, a friend, colleague and popular *Inquirer* columnist who wrote this book's Foreword. My deepest appreciation goes to David Milne, assistant managing editor/design, Gary Haynes, former assistant managing editor/graphics, and Clem Murray, director of photography, who spent many hours editing, designing, and helping me shape this book.

Special thanks, too, to Lois Wark, assistant managing editor; Constance Pickett and the staff of the News Research Library of Philadelphia Newspapers Inc., and George Brightbill of Temple University Urban Archives.

FOREWORD

Six days after a feisty little guy named Harry S. Truman upset heavily favored Tom Dewey in the 1948 presidential election, an equally feisty guy, name of Michael Viola, joined the staff of *The Philadelphia Inquirer.*

They both turned out to be good ones.

Mike Viola, especially.

Viola went on to become a photographer of purest ray serene, a master of his art, a star who nonetheless has always been the quintessential team player.

During his 40 years with *The Inquirer*, Michael Viola received more applause than a Rotary luncheon. Indeed, from the time he went "on the street" with his camera in 1964 until he retired in 1988, there never was a year in which he did not win at least one major award for his photography.

It may have been the longest winning streak since Alexander the Great.

A native South Philadelphian who grew up in Texas, of all places, Viola joined *The Inquirer* staff in November 1948, fresh out of the Navy. He had served aboard a cruiser during World War II, eventually becoming ship's photographer. In 1946, he helped set up the remote photo apparatus for the first atomic bomb tests at Bikini atoll in the Marshall Islands.

He began—at $28 a week—as an inside printer, a situation akin to a promising young ballplayer's starting with a team as batboy, just to get a foot in the door. It was to be an apprenticeship of considerable duration.

Once on the street, though, Viola quickly made his mark. During the North Philadelphia riots in September 1964, he made a photograph that was picked up from *The Inquirer* by the Associated Press and sent throughout the world. It showed four black women, amid the shambles of shattered peace spread by the riots, serving coffee and food to five policemen, four white and one black.

In one black and white photograph, the sensitivity of Michael Viola was delineated for all the world to see.

During his career, Viola has covered just about every type of news event. He has covered sports (in 1969, he stopped a line drive by Phillies' slugger Rich Allen, blasted from 90 feet away, with his chest, astonishingly suffering only a bad bruise) and he has made superb fashion photographs. In 1977 he was sent to Rome to cover the canonization of St. John Neumann.

A compleat professional.

For more than 15 years, it was my privilege to work many an assignment with Michael Viola. He, of course, was the photo man and I was the workman, and right from the start we clicked as a team. There was a compatibility there that stood us both in good stead. In fact, colleagues obviously conversant with the Batman patios hung the tag "Dynamic Duo" on us.

So let me tell you about Michael Viola. Let me tell you what it's like to work regularly with a little-heralded—until now—genius.

First off, when you're a reporter/writer working with Mike, it is necessary that you always expect the unexpected. If you don't, you are odds-on to become a candidate for admission to a funny farm.

Unlike many another photographer/reporter team whose members go their separate ways to an assignment, Mike and I almost always traveled to the site together. En route to the assignment site we would talk about the story, discussing the principals and the possibilities for unusual photographs that would point up the theme.

Thus was formulated our game plan.

Once on site, we made changes in our proposed procedures—often without consulting each other. While I, say, would be in one location, conducting an interview, Viola would spot an opportunity to make a photograph that we hadn't discussed en route to the job, but one that would add to the package we would be taking back to the office. He would make the photograph and tell me about it later. Or I would switch off from one interview to another, making the happy discovery that Mike was right behind me.

There comes to mind the day we were assigned to cover the funeral of a small girl who had been abducted, raped and finally murdered. En route to the funeral home we spoke of how vital it was that we blend into the background, attracting as little attention as possible.

The funeral home was filled with mourners, and at one end stood a tiny casket in which reposed the child's body. Banked around the casket were flowers in profusion.

Viola moved about, using high-speed film to snap photographs, thus rendering unnecessary the use of artificial light. Then, suddenly, Mike apparently disappeared. We had discussed nothing like this, so for a time I had no idea of where he might be.

It turned out that he wanted to photograph the girl's mother as she bent over the child for a last goodbye just before the casket was to be closed. And the only way for him to get the proper angle was to move into the bank of flowers immediately behind the head of the casket. He moved in unobtrusively, made his photograph and moved out. I believe that no one—including me—realized what had occurred.

The photograph that Mike made that day was one of the masterpieces of his career.

It is important to note that Viola was impeccably dressed that day, as he was every day when he reported for work. Wearing a suit and tie on the job was a must for him. "You never know where you may have to go," he would explain.

During the Bicentennial observance in 1976, we put together a story on Carpenters Hall in Philadelphia, the meeting place of the First Continental Congress in 1774. The live-in caretakers of the building were a husband and wife who claimed that every so often there issued from the attic sounds of a vigorous debate. And on less frequent occasions they heard a voice, which they figured had to be that of Patrick Henry, thundering "Give me liberty, or give me death!"

While I did the interview, Mike made various shots of the couple and the hall, but it was apparent that he wanted something more. Suddenly, he excused himself and left Carpenter Hall. When he returned, he was carrying a thick glass ashtray.

"I am," he told the couple, "going to turn you into a couple of ghosts." Then, shooting through the bottom of the ashtray, he made a ghostly-looking picture that was practically enough to convince readers that Patrick Henry was, indeed, sounding off in the attic of Carpenters Hall.

Michael Viola is the photographer who in 1967 staked out a vantage point outside Philadelphia's Convention Hall that would enable him to get an exclusive photograph of Frank Sinatra, to the immense displeasure of the singer's bodyguards. There were threats, but Viola held his ground and got his photograph, which made Page 1 the next day. And when Frank Rizzo, then the commissioner of police, heard about the fuss, he sent word to Sinatra that if anything untoward happened to Viola, he (Rizzo) would throw Sinatra's entire entourage into the slammer.

Michael Viola also is the man who in 1980 accompanied me to the Veterinary Hospital of the University of Pennsylvania, where we were to do a story on a dog named Lady. The dog had been caught in an illegal trap set in Fairmount Park, and there was every likelihood that her right front paw would have to be amputated. And within minutes after our arrival, there was Michael Viola, sprawled on the floor, photographing the sad-eyed Lady.

Eventually, the dog's leg was amputated and she was sent home. Some six months later, we did a follow-up. The three-legged Lady, considerably more cheerful than when we first had seen her, greeted us. And what did Michael Viola do?" He sprawled on the floor and began making pictures.

There is, of course, no way that I can find words that do justice to Michael Viola's pictures. So-o-o-

As they used to say in Vaudeville, I've been on long enough. Just take it from me that Viola has put together a book I am sure you will enjoy. If you want to curl up with a good book, start curling and turn this page.

Edgar Williams

Columnist for *The Philadelphia Inquirer*

CONTENTS

Dedicated To
The Memory Of My Beloved Granddaughter
Jaclyn Ann Kurcik

PUBLISHED FRIDAY, FEBRUARY 20, 1987

During a stormy debate, Councilman John Street (left) lashes out at Councilwoman Joan L. Krajewski (far right) after she opposes a $600,000 grant for a youth-training program run by civic leader Samuel L. Evans, making it the largest grant approved for a single group in recent city history. Krajewski in arguing against the bill, said the transfer of $600,000 was unreasonable "at a time when we face a $40 million deficit, when recreation centers do without maintenance and when libraries are unstaffed and threatened with shorter hours, when potholes go unfilled. We cannot send this kind of signal to the taxpayers of Philadelphia."
UPDATE: Former City Councilman John. F. Street took over as Council President January 6, 1992.

MOVE members outside MOVE headquarters, 309 N. 33d Street, as Philadelphia police survey area near Pearl Street. A controversy grew over MOVE's first headquarters when neighbors complained of odors from garbage and human and animal excrement, as well as the presence of rats. Members put up a tall fence around the site and built a high stage behind it. Tensions were high in early 1977 when a half-dozen MOVE members brandished rifles from atop the stage. On command by Mayor Frank L. Rizzo, police threw a blockade around the property, winning the authority from a judge after the city cited unpaid water and gas bills and MOVE's refusal to permit inspection of its property. On August 8, 1978, police took the property by force, attempting to serve arrest warrants for 21 MOVE members. Gunfire broke out and Officer James J. Ramp was shot dead. After a chaotic, obscenity-filled trial, nine MOVE members— five men, four women—were sentenced to 30 to 100 years in prison each.

PUBLISHED SUNDAY, JULY 17, 1977

MOVE headquarters at 309 N. 33d Street in East Powelton Village

PUBLISHED FRIDAY, MARCH 17, 1978

A policeman, behind sandbags and a shield inside an abandoned building, watches the MOVE house.

PUBLISHED FRIDAY, MAY 9, 1980

MOVE supporters scream insults in Common Pleas Court after all nine MOVE members were found guilty of third-degree murder in the 1978 shooting of police officer James Ramp, ending the longest and costliest trial in the history of Philadelphia's criminal court system. Each of the five male and four female defendants were also found guilty of attempted murder, conspiracy and seven charges of aggravated assault.

UPDATE: On August 4, 1981, nine MOVE members were sentenced to prison terms of 30 to 100 years for the 1978 shootout when police officer James J. Ramp was killed, three police officers and firefighters were wounded. However, MOVE members contended that they fired no shots.

Relatives comfort Olithia Dotson Tillman, an aunt of Katricia and Zanetta Dotson Africa, teenage half-sisters believed to have perished in the MOVE fire on Osage Avenue in West Philadelphia in which 11 people died, 5 of them children, 61 homes destroyed and 250 people left homeless in the 2nd MOVE confrontation on May 13, 1985. Tillman's daughter Vanessa (left) mourns by herself. About 40 people attended the funeral service held at the Emanuel Lutheran Church at Fourth and Carpenter Streets in Philadelphia.

PUBLISHED WEDNESDAY, APRIL 15, 1987

Fending off reporters, Mayor W. Wilson Goode walks down a City Hall corridor on his way to appear before the Philadelphia grand jury investigating the May 1985 MOVE confrontation. The mayor spent more than five hours testifying about the incident, in which 11 people died, 61 homes were destroyed and 250 people were left homeless. The timing of his order to put out the fire was expected to be a focus of the grand jury's questioning.

5

PUBLISHED FRIDAY, MARCH 7, 1986

The MOVE commission formally released its report at a televised news conference, with commission chairman William H. Brown 3d telling the citizens of Philadelphia, "The rest is up to you." Airing its findings at station WHYY-TV, the Special Investigation Commission, (from left) Charles W. Bowser; M. Todd Cooke; Charisse R. Lillie; H. Graham McDonald; William B. Lytton 3d; William H. Brown 3d; Carl E. Singley; Julia M. Chinn; Msgr. Edward P. Cullen; Rev. Audrey F. Bronson; Bruce W. Kauffman and Rev. Paul Washington.

UPDATE: A city investigating Grand Jury exonerated city officials and employees of criminal wrongdoing in the May 13, 1985 MOVE debacle, in which eleven people in the radical group's fortified rowhouse, five of them children, died when police dropped a bomb on the house at 6221 Osage Avenue in West Philadelphia. The bomb ignited a fire that destroyed 61 homes and left 250 people homeless.

PUBLISHED THURSDAY, OCTOBER 31, 1985

Fire Commissioner William C. Richmond, in the course of his long and emotional testimony before the Philadelphia Special Investigation Commission on MOVE. During the May 13 MOVE confrontation, 11 MOVE members were killed and 61 homes were destroyed by fire.

PUBLISHED FRIDAY, MAY 8, 1987

After turning himself in on theft and conspiracy charges, developer Ernest A. Edwards Jr. is led to a police van. Edwards and his former business partner, W. Oscar Harris Jr., surrendered after their indictment on charges that they stole a total of $208,112 during the rebuilding of 61 houses destroyed in the May 13, 1985 MOVE confrontation. UPDATE: Convicted of stealing more than $137,000 in his failed attempt to rebuild the 61 houses, Edwards was sentenced October 27, 1988 to seven to 14 years in state prison and ordered to repay the money he was convicted of taking. Edwards insisted during the 4½ hour sentencing hearing that he was innocent of any crime.

PUBLISHED WEDNESDAY, AUGUST 21, 1985

Laying a foundation for a new house on the 6200 block of Osage Avenue, a worker smoothes cement around some cinder blocks. The house is one of those being built to replace the 61 destroyed by fire during the city's confrontation with MOVE in West Philadelphia May 13, which also left 11 people dead.

PUBLISHED SATURDAY, NOVEMBER 12, 1983

Dozens of veterans in dress uniforms and fatigues, saluted America's war dead and military personnel during Veterans Day ceremonies at Washington Square and other locations throughout Philadelphia. Vietnam veteran Joseph Petti bows his head during memorial ceremony in Washington Square.

PUBLISHED TUESDAY, JANUARY 7, 1969

Pfc. Donald G. Smith, 21, one of three Americans released on New Year's Day after more than eight months imprisonment by the Vietcong, is reunited with his parents, Mr. And Mrs. Donald R. Smith, and his brother, Kirby, 14, at Valley Forge General Hospital. The Smith family, from Akron in Lancaster County, drove to the hospital to await him. Asked if he ever lost hope of being freed, Smith said, "No, I just kept hoping." What did he miss most? "My freedom," he replied.

SATURDAY, APRIL 5, 1969

In a solemn antiwar protest, the names of the American war dead in Vietnam were being read at the Philadelphia center-city draft headquarters. The demonstration was expected to last more than 15 hours during the reading of the names of 31,179 victims of the war taken from a list published in the Congressional Record.

PUBLISHED THURSDAY, JUNE 11, 1987

Rescue workers use a life-support line as they search the Crosswicks Creek in Bordentown Township, N. J., for the bodies of three Trenton boys missing and presumed drowned. The body of one of the boys was found. The three had been on an outing at their teacher's house when they disappeared. The search was conducted by volunteers from Burlington and Mercer Counties and state police.

PUBLISHED THURSDAY, MARCH 31, 1977

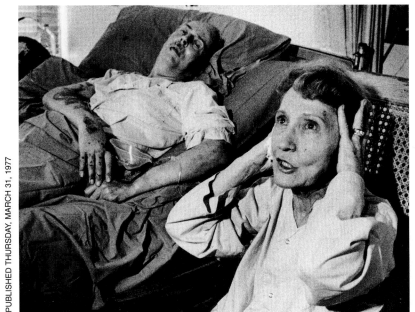

PUBLISHED MONDAY, AUGUST 28, 1967

PUBLISHED FRIDAY, OCTOBER 3, 1969

Fifty-three airline survivors ended a long painful odyssey across an ocean after their expensive holiday abroad ended in the worst airline disaster in history. Five hundred and seventy seven passengers died when a KLM Royal Dutch Airline Boeing 747 rammed a Pan American World Airways 747 at Los Rodeos Airport on the Island of Tenerife. Some of the survivors told their stories at Walson Army Hospital near Fort Dix, N. J. Her hands on her head, Florence Trumbell relives the crash as her husband, Albert, lies beside her.

Army Captain Ralph Perkins, of Magee Avenue, returning from Vietnam, meets his wife, Jean, and sons, Chip, 21 months, and Michael, 8 ½ months, whom he had never seen, at Philadelphia International Airport.

Matthew Lamelza, holding the Silver Star awarded posthumously to his son Mario, weeps as his wife is comforted by Major Thomas Murotore of the Army Advisory Defense Supply Agency. Pvt. Lamelza was killed in Vietnam. The medal was presented at the Lamelza home on N. 7th Street, Philadelphia.

PUBLISHED FRIDAY, JUNE 23, 1978

With bodies of victims nearby under sheets, a federal aviation official studies the wreckage of a twin-engine plane that was bound for a Chicago convention and crashed in a muddy cornfield moments after takeoff from the Pottstown-Limerick Airport in Montgomery County. Witnesses said the plane burst into flames and exploded as it hit the ground, flipped and broke apart, skidding into a line of trees 400 feet north of the intersection of Lightcap and Possum Hollow Roads. "It was like an inferno."

PUBLISHED SATURDAY, JUNE 7, 1975

Railroad officials investigate a railroad crossing accident that killed three persons aboard a Reading Co. train as it was going from West Trenton, N. J. to the Reading terminal in center city Philadelphia. The dead were James J. Doyle Jr., 50, of Philadelphia, the train's engineer; John F. Conway, 46, of Glenolden, the trainman; and the only passenger, Nancy T. Griffin, 27, of Rockledge. When the train smashed into the trailer, one of the eight-ton rolls and a five-ton roll were thrown into the front of the railroad car, protruding halfway into it.

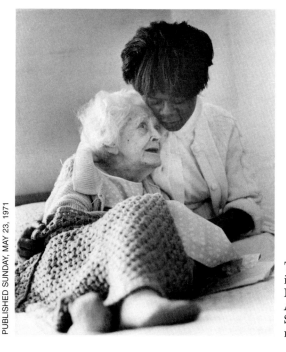

PUBLISHED SUNDAY, MAY 23, 1971

The need for human warmth runs strong in homes for the aged. At Sacred Heart Manor in Germantown, Philadelphia, Mrs. Anna Miller, who will be 100 on September 15th, gets reassurance from nurses' aide Diane Bridges.

PUBLISHED THURSDAY, MARCH 4, 1965

Bruce Bateman, an Oakmont fireman, takes a spectacular spill after walking out of a fire-damaged pet shop, at 609 Lancaster Avenue, Wynnewood, Pa., with an armload of records and valuables to be stored for safekeeping. Others look on in amazement.

PUBLISHED TUESDAY, NOVEMBER 4, 1986

Amid the pipes, David Casso, an organ society member and a senior at Penn, was among several other pipe-organ buffs talking about the just completed restoration of one of Philadelphia's greatest musical treasures: the 10,731-pipe Curtis Organ. It began life in 1926 at the International Sesquicentennial Exposition, but for the last 58 years it has been in the Irving Auditorium on the campus of the University of Pennsylvania. The restoration took nearly seven years and considerable labor by a group of about 75 buffs called the Curtis Organ Restoration Society, which has the university's official blessing and is a mixture of Penn personnel and people from various outside pursuits. For all concerned, it was a labor of love. Not only did the participants receive no more than psychic reward, but they also helped raise the necessary money for materials.

PUBLISHED SATURDAY, JULY 22, 1978

In a pool is where Helen Huffman's car wound up as she drove through the Valley Forge National Historical Park, and she tells National Park Service officials how it happened. Miss Huffman, who works for the park service, was driving up a hill on an unfamiliar dirt road. The road had been closed and there were no signs indicating that a pool was at the top of the hill. She was treated at Sacred Heart Hospital in Norristown, Pa. and released.

PUBLISHED SUNDAY, APRIL 4, 1976

Finishing his budget message Philadelphia Mayor Frank L. Rizzo is applauded by Council member (from left) Council President George X. Schwartz at the podium (background), Anna C. Verna, Joseph Coleman and Beatrice Chernock. The Mayor proposed a $1.3 billion city budget for the 1976-77 fiscal year that calls for an increase in the wage tax to 4 percent and layoffs of between 500 and 1,000 non-uniformed city workers. Rizzo also asked the City Council to approve five other tax increases, including a 29.3 percent increase in the real estate tax. That proposal is the key element to the city's emergency tax package that has been stalled in the State Legislature since January. In his presentation to the City Council, the mayor said, "Philadelphians are prepared to bite the bullet."

PUBLISHED SUNDAY, MAY 30, 1976

Selling with their fists, several of the city's street vendors clashed with police during a demonstration in the City Council chambers. The Philadelphia vendors were protesting new restrictive ordinances governing their peddling business. The ordinances were passed 13-3 and 10 vendors were arrested in the disturbance.

PUBLISHED SATURDAY, AUGUST 13, 1977

Angry protesters try to force their way into the State Office Building at Broad and Spring Garden Streets, in Philadelphia, as state security officers stressfully try to force the glass door closed. The demonstrators were among thousands of welfare workers who staged noisy demonstrations in Philadelphia and in Harrisburg over the budget impasse.

UPDATE: The Pennsylvania House of Representatives narrowly approved a new state budget early August 20, ending the long divisive fight that had paralyzed the Legislature for seven weeks.

PUBLISHED MONDAY, AUGUST 21, 1967

According to rites of the Neo-American Church, hippies Merri Baldus, 21, and Michael Christopher, 23, are married by an ornately dressed Boo Hoo of the church on the east plaza of the Philadelphia Museum of Art. It was the first such ceremony in Philadelphia for the flower people, and some 75 persons were there to see it. The bride said the green in her dress stood for fertility and the blue for love. The groom paid the marriage fee with a large white rooster.

PUBLISHED SUNDAY, OCTOBER 24, 1971

It's Jesus who turns them on. While his parents hold hands with other believers at Long Beach Island, New Jersey, a toddler's eye is caught by some less serious activity. Philadelphia's self-proclaimed "Jesus Freaks" are putting down drugs and pushing a new kind of spiritual high, old-time religion. Jesus People like their services simple, robust and emotional. They wander where the spirit leads.

17

PUBLISHED FRIDAY, JUNE 12, 1987

Frameworks for improvement stand in contrast as work remains to be done at the edge of Center City's skyline. At 940 feet, the new One Liberty Place (left) is Philadelphia's tallest building, having taken that distinction from the 548-foot City Hall, where work is to resume on the tower and the William Penn statue atop it. During a restoration that began in 1986, the original iron skin of the statue was replaced by a skin of 2,000 steel plates. Penn also received a cleaning and waxing. The restoration of the statue and the top 210 feet of the tower, which was completed in 1991, cost a total of $25 million.

PUBLISHED THURSDAY, MAY 28, 1987

The 12-ton 146-foot spire for One Liberty Place, Philadelphia's tallest building, is set in place in a ceremony in which the final section of the spire was lifted atop the 940-foot building.

PUBLISHED FRIDAY, APRIL 11, 1980

William L. McLean 3d, *Bulletin* editor and publisher (left), and Karl Eller, chairman of Charter Media Co. of Phoenix, Ariz., chat before meeting with the *Bulletin* staff to explain the purchase of the *Bulletin*, and what it will mean. The *Bulletin*, a locally owned institution for more than 130 years and Philadelphia's largest weekday newspaper, is being sold to Charter Media Co., for an undisclosed sum of cash and notes.
UPDATE: The *Bulletin*, whose famous slogan was that nearly everybody read it, ceased publication Friday, January 29, 1982, ending an era of distinguished journalism that had its beginnings 134 years ago.

PUBLISHED FRIDAY, APRIL 11, 1980

Karl Eller (right) chairman of Charter Media Co. of Phoenix, Ariz., explains the purchase of the *Bulletin*, and what it will mean, to the assembled staff members.

PUBLISHED SATURDAY JANUARY 29, 1983

On January 29, 1982, the *Bulletin* ceased publication, ending an era of distinguished journalism that began in 1848. One thing that keeps the memory of the newspaper alive is the plenitude of sidewalk newsstands throughout the city that still display the famous slogan, "Nearly Everybody Reads The *Bulletin*." The one pictured is owned and operated by Fanny Kliger, 79, who said that she has kept the *Bulletin* sign on the stand for auld lang syne. "I was really sorry to see the *Bulletin* go," Mrs. Kliger said. "I liked it better than *The Inquirer*."

PUBLISHED TUESDAY, OCTOBER 9, 1979

Upon his arrival in Philadelphia, Wednesday, October 3, 1979, hundreds of thousands of people poured into Broad Street and the Benjamin Franklin Parkway to see and hear Pope John Paul II. At the Wednesday evening Mass on the Parkway, more than a million people waited outside the Cathedral of SS. Peter and Paul and Logan Circle, where the Pope began the ancient and solemn ritual of the Eucharist. At the Civic Center, Thursday October 4, John Paul II and about 200 concelebrants said Mass before 15,000 priests and nuns from every diocese in the country. Afterward he blessed 15 young patients who had been brought from Children's Hospital to see him, then departed for the airport, where 2,200 school girls waited to sing him a farewell. Before stepping into the plane, the Pope paused to shake hands with 20 police officers who were standing guard. Then, just a day after he had arrived, he left Philadelphia for the rest of his American journey.

PUBLISHED TUESDAY, OCTOBER 9, 1979

When he stepped from his jetliner at Philadelphia International Airport, Wednesday, October 3, 1979, Pope John Paul II was greeted by a friend of 20 years, John Cardinal Krol, and by Mayor Frank L. Rizzo and other dignitaries. Hundreds of thousands of people poured onto Broad Street and the Benjamin Franklin Parkway to see and hear him. "God bless Philadelphia," the Pope told the congregation in the Cathedral of SS. Peter and Paul, declaring the "City of Brotherly Love" to be "a symbol of freedom and fraternal relations."

PUBLISHED MONDAY, AUGUST 31, 1964

Philadelphia residents of the 1600 block on Norris Street serving free coffee to policemen on riot control duty in the neighborhood. At the time, further rioting seemed an imminent danger, and it was largely because of the spirit of these and numerous other Negro residents that calm was restored and the voices of reason prevailed.

PUBLISHED FRIDAY, OCTOBER 30, 1981

State police troopers waiting inside Graterford Prison in Montgomery County as a group of four to ten armed prisoners holds 38 hostages in the kitchen area of the prison. Prison officials and psychiatrists were talking with the inmates, but said no solution was in sight. They said that none of the hostages or inmates had been injured, and that the inmates holding the hostages had issued no demands even after they were asked specifically if there were any. A group of four to ten inmates, who entered the kitchen after a foiled escape attempt Wednesday night, were holding three prison guards, three civilian food services workers and 32 inmates who were working in the kitchen, authorities said. The inmates were armed with at least one handgun, officials said, and they have access to several knives and other potential weapons in the kitchen area.

UPDATE: A group of armed inmates holding six staff members hostage, released their captives unharmed and surrendered, ending their five-day siege peacefully, November 2, 1981.

PUBLISHED FRIDAY, JUNE 6, 1986

Standing over the hats of officers Daniel Gleason and his partner Laurine Venable, two police officers survey the shooting scene where Officer Gleason was killed when he was shot in the face at point-blank range while trying to break up a fight in North Philadelphia between prostitutes and a resident upset about neighborhood crime, police said. Officer Daniel Gleason, 39, the father of six children, was rushed to Temple University Hospital. He was pronounced dead about an hour after the shooting. The resident, Nathan Long, 38, was shot twice in the arm by Gleason's partner, Officer Laurine Venable. Police said Long drove himself to Temple University Hospital and staggered to the door trailing blood before he was treated, arrested and charged with murder.

UPDATE: Nathan Long, 39, was convicted by a Common Pleas Court jury November 28, 1986, of first-degree murder in the slaying of Philadelphia police Officer Daniel Gleason on June 5. Long was sentenced to life in prison November 29, 1986.

PUBLISHED SATURDAY, JUNE 16, 1984

At Resurrection Cemetery, members of Engine Company No. 25 lift the casket bearing fellow firefighter Joseph L. Konrad Jr., 37, from a fire truck. Konrad, who died in the line of duty, was killed in the blazing collapse of a vacant Fishtown rowhouse, which had been cited by the city as a public nuisance.

PUBLISHED THURSDAY, OCTOBER 2, 1980

A somber procession leaves the Immaculate Heart of Mary Church in Roxborough after services for Philadelphia police officer Garrett Farrell, killed in a shootout with a suspected purse-snatcher. Among the mourners are Farrell's brothers William (top left) and Michael (top right), both officers; his sister, Robyn (in front of William); his wife, Stephanie (center), an officer, and at her left, his mother, Mary. Farrell, 25, a strapping, good-natured, athletic man, was one of four officers from the same family assigned to the city's 14th Police District. The purse-snatching suspect, Chester Tann, who had a lengthy police record, was shot and killed by officer Farrell's partner William J. Mock, who was shot in the same incident.

PUBLISHED SATURDAY, SEPTEMBER 26, 1987

Elizabeth McCarthy weeps as she clutches the flag that draped the casket of her husband, Mounted Police Officer William D. McCarthy. McCarthy was killed in the line of duty on Broad Street near Pattison Avenue when he and his horse, Skipper, were struck by a truck driven by an off-duty Philadelphia police officer. The officer, Charles Loughran, 39, has been charged with vehicular homicide and drunken driving. McCarthy, a 10-year veteran of the force, was given a hero's funeral, filled with drama and ceremony, at Holy Sepulchre Cemetery.

PUBLISHED SATURDAY, AUGUST 12, 1978

James Ramp Jr. comforts his mother as they follow the casket out of St. Dominic's Roman Catholic Church. The hundreds who came to St. Dominic's Roman Catholic Church to pay last respects to Philadelphia policeman James J. Ramp learned for the first time that he had lost his life while going to the aid of a wounded fellow officer. The Rt. Rev. Msgr. Charles Devlin, who delivered the eulogy during a Mass of Christian Burial for Officer Ramp, told the 800 mourners that the officer had been shot attempting to reach a comrade who had been hit Tuesday during the bloody firefight between the police and the radical group MOVE.

PUBLISHED THURSDAY, JULY 1, 1976

Attending services at Holy Innocents Church for slain Officer Walter L. Szwajkowski are (from left) family friend Francis Clarke, Fire Commissioner Joseph Rizzo, Mayor Frank L. Rizzo, Police Commissioner Joseph F. O'Neill and City Managing Director Hillel Levinson. Szwajkowski, 45, of the 35th Police District, a 22-year veteran of the force was killed when he was summoned from the Nativity of the Blessed Virgin Church, Belgrade Street and Allegheny Avenue, in Philadelphia, where he was attending Mass, to subdue a man who had forced four persons from their car when they stopped for a traffic light outside the church. His alleged killer Leon Harasimowicz, died a half hour later at Northeastern Hospital.

PUBLISHED WEDNESDAY, NOVEMBER 5, 1975

Ms. Joanne Barnes weeps at the casket of her 7-year-old daughter, Virginia Caldwell, who was raped and murdered. Virginia, who was reported missing from her home at North 22d Street in Philadelphia, was found dead on a grass plot at the Raymond Rosen Housing Project, 23d and Diamond Streets. Approximately 250 persons attended services for the child, who was eulogized as a "beautiful flower" who is now in Paradise. The mourners were urged to "do something about rooting out the evil in our sick society before the time comes for each of us to stand in judgment before God."
UPDATE: John Davis, 36, an unemployed tailor, accused of murdering Virginia Caldwell on October 29, 1975, pleaded guilty in October 1976, after sitting through his trial for seven days. Davis was convicted of first-degree murder. A mandatory sentence of life in prison would be set at a later date.

On a hill in Manayunk, Ursula Jones, oblivious to the scene behind her, sweeps snow in front of her house on Terrace street. The snowstorm with driving winds brought the region to a virtual standstill, closing schools, offices, banks and business. Pennsylvania Governor Milton J. Shapp proclaimed a state of extreme emergency, making the National Guard available for rescue operation.

With the East River Drive below and nowhere to go, one of three city trash collectors wearing a safety harness attached to ropes, eases his way from the truck as fire rescue personnel prepare to pull him to safety. The three Philadelphia trash collectors spent about 40 minutes dangling 100 feet above the East River Drive after their truck crashed part-way through a guardrail on the twin bridges of the Schuylkill Expressway's Roosevelt Extension. The three trash collectors were taken to Osteopathic Hospital, where they were treated for minor injuries.

PUBLISHED THURSDAY, NOVEMBER 5, 1987

On Tuesday night, a proud and defiant Frank L. Rizzo declared he would never concede to Philadelphia Mayor W. Wilson Goode. Yesterday, a far more humble and subdued Rizzo seemed closer to accepting defeat in what he has called his final run for office. "I'm a little disgusted that I lost, but I tell you, I'm proud of what I accomplished." Surrounded by his aides, Rizzo offered as his greatest disappointment that he had failed his supporters by not winning. "You know, the toughest part of this for me personally," he said, "I've made my mark. I've been around. I have nothing I want or need. And so I feel bad for the people who gave their very best, young people, black and white. People who gave me money. I let them down...I was disappointed. I feel bad, sure," he said. "But for the people who helped me, I didn't deliver for them, and I feel awful for them."
UPDATE: Frank L. Rizzo, 70, who dominated the city of Philadelphia as politician, policeman and mayor, died July 16, 1991.

PUBLISHED FRIDAY, JULY 18, 1986

Throwing trash across the driveway, strikers temporarily block the entrance to the Northwest Incinerator, in Philadelphia. The city sanitation workers refused to return to work as ordered by a Common Pleas Court judge. The strike entered its 17th day.

UPDATE: Striking blue-collar workers voted July 20, at an emotional and divided general membership meeting, to return to work without a new contract. The vote by a majority of about 2,500 members of District Council 33 of the American Federation of State, County and Municipal Employees (AFSCME) ended a 20-day old strike that had halted trash collection and disrupted numerous other city services.

Rain-soaked members of the Ku Klux Klan near burning 30-foot cross in a field in East Nottingham township, Chester County. It was the Klan's first major Pennsylvania rally in 30 years. Less than a dozen of those in attendance wore the familiar white linen robes and hoods of the Klan.

PUBLISHED SATURDAY, APRIL 22, 1978

SCORE

STOP
Forced
Busing

PUBLISHED THURSDAY, JULY 2, 1987

In a scuffle outside Temple University Hospital, a striker (right) grapples with a man who said he was trying to visit a patient. The incident occurred before a court ordered strikers to stop blocking hospital entrances. Later 46 people were arrested.
UPDATE: A tentative agreement was reached July 1, 1987, in the one-day old strike by clerical and health-care workers at Temple University and Temple University Hospital.

U.S. District Judge Murray Schwartz was honored at the Hotel DuPont by a Wilmington civic group, while about 50 demonstrators stood across the street picketing and jeering. Schwartz became Delaware's most controversial, most vilified citizen last year after he issued an order requiring large-scale busing to desegregate the Wilmington and New Castle County schools. A woman protester with placard 'Stop Forced Busing' had a few words for the judge, as a flag waves from her hand on her head.

31

PUBLISHED SATURDAY, MARCH 26, 1977

No effort was made to settle the day-old Transport Workers Union strike which had idled the city transit division's trains, buses and trolleys for the second time in two years, leaving 400,000 SEPTA riders stranded. At Overbrook Station, a large crowd of commuters trying to catch a ride into town watched train after train, already loaded at outlying stops, whisk by them.
UPDATE: The bitter 44-day Philadelphia transit strike ended May 7, 1977 with the announcement that members of the Transport Workers Union had approved SEPTA's offer for a two-year contract settlement.

PUBLISHED SATURDAY, OCTOBER 8, 1977

James E. Nelson of Wenonah, N. J., a member of the Non-Resident Taxpayers Association (NRTA) exposing his anti-tax message with a group of disgruntled New Jersey taxpayers who marched to Woodbury, N. J., to criticize what they consider a modern-day version of taxation without representation: the Philadelphia city wage tax. About 200 people, some shouting "no taxation without representation," paraded in front of the office of a lawyer who had been hired by the City of Philadelphia to collect default judgments against New Jersey residents who have refused to pay the wage tax. All non-Philadelphia residents who work in the city are required to pay the same city wage tax as are Philadelphia residents.

Asked by striking picket why she was crossing the picket line at the School Administration Building, 21st and the Parkway, the school administration employee's response was a short one. Philadelphia teachers went on strike September 8th., demanding that their contract, broken during the worst school budget crisis in years, be honored in full. The 50-day school strike ended October 27, and a scheduled city-wide general strike was averted.

33

PUBLISHED THURSDAY, JULY 13, 1978

District Council 33's president Earl Stout (left) with secretary treasurer Ron Smith, on brink of a strike. Philadelphia contract negotiations with 19,500 non-uniformed city employees, more than 17,000 of them represented by Stout, approached a strike deadline. UPDATE: The largest municipal strike in Philadelphia history ended on its eighth day July 21, 1978 when non-uniformed city workers voted to accept a controversial two-year contract.

PUBLISHED MONDAY, MARCH 29, 1971

The Rev. Carl McIntire debates with Homophile group of 20 men and women from the Philadelphia based Homophile Action League, demanding that the pastor (left) of Collingswood's Bible Presbyterian Church grant them equal time on radio station WXUR in Media, Pa., to answer the minister's statements on "corruption" of homosexuals. During the demonstration, Mr. McIntire repeatedly asked the pickets to come into the church. "I love young people," Mr. McIntire said, "I love you. I want to help you to hear what we say. I have the message that can help you."
UPDATE: The station, WXUR went off the air in 1973, when the FCC ruled that Rev. Carl McIntire had not given equal air time to those with opposing viewpoints and that he had not fulfilled promises made to the FCC when he bought the station in Media, Pa.

PUBLISHED WEDNESDAY, OCTOBER 1, 1975

If Ron Zauner had been picketing alone against the Greyhound Bus Co. for losing one of his packages on a transcontinental shipment, he might not have gotten the attention or sympathy he received by calling his pet puppy into service as a picket with placard "It hurts to be screwed by a Greyhound."

PUBLISHED THURSDAY, AUGUST 6, 1981

Picnicking with their families in Roosevelt Park near the airport, Philadelphia air traffic controllers mark their firings by the President with a cheer at the hour of Reagan's deadline. The Reagan administration began firing striking controllers and declared that it was ready to run the nation's airports without them, even though it would be "no cakewalk" for the flying public over the next year or two. Neither the government nor the Professional Air Traffic Controllers Organization budged from their hard-line stands in the walkout by about 13,000 union controllers.

PUBLISHED SUNDAY, MARCH 7, 1976

A women's march in support of the Equal Rights Amendment is led by Karen DeCrow (in fur coat), president of the National Organization for Women. The march, part of an advance celebration of International Women's Day, was held in Philadelphia, beginning at City Hall and continuing to the Unitarian Church at 21st and Chestnut Streets.

PUBLISHED THURSDAY, OCTOBER 10, 1974

Key provisions of the state's new abortion law were temporarily blocked by a Federal judge in Pittsburgh as a special three-judge panel in Philadelphia began hearing arguments by attorneys for Planned Parenthood and other pro-abortion groups to have the entire law overturned. As the judges were assembling, about 25 pickets from various other groups marched outside the 9th and Chestnut Street Federal Courthouse waving and carrying signs that said such things as "Hands Off My Body," and "Defend a Women's Right to Choose."

PUBLISHED TUESDAY, JULY 25, 1978

Lee Frissell, of the Consumer Party is ejected after he refused to leave when ruled out of order during Philadelphia City Council agenda hearings which called for testimony on an amendment to the City Charter that would allow Mayor Frank L. Rizzo to seek a third term in office. Frissell dumped on the speaker's table petitions that he said were signed by 30,000 persons opposed to the third-term amendment. Council President George X. Schwartz cautioned him, as he did all speakers, against direct testimony about the talents of Rizzo.

UPDATE: By a 2-1 ratio, Philadelphians on November 7, 1978 destroyed Frank L. Rizzo's hopes for a third consecutive term as mayor. Voters rejected Rizzo's proposal to remove the two-term mayoral limit from the City Charter with a resounding "no" vote. Rizzo conceded defeat in a brief statement to his disconsolate supporters at the Benjamin Franklin Hotel. "You win some, you lose some; you have to accept defeat with a smile," said Rizzo, 58, who never before had been repudiated at the polls. "I want to thank everyone from the bottom of my heart."

PUBLISHED WEDNESDAY, NOVEMBER 8, 1978

Philadelphia voters turned out in heavy, possibly record numbers, to settle a bitter controversy over a City Charter amendment that could allow Mayor Frank L. Rizzo to run for a third successive term. Rizzo (top right), the center of the controversy, predicted a victory for the charter change when he entered the polling place in the Seventh Day Adventist Church, Germantown and Rex Avenues. As he entered the stone building, he was flanked by large signs reading, "No on Charter Change" and "Vote Yes on Charter Reform." UPDATE: By a 2-1 ratio, Philadelphians on November 7, 1978, destroyed Frank L. Rizzo's hopes for a third consecutive term as mayor. Voters rejected Rizzo's proposal to remove the two-term mayoral limit from the City Charter with a resounding "no" vote.

PUBLISHED TUESDAY, JULY 25, 1978

Philadelphia City Council agenda hearings which called for testimony on an amendment to the City Charter that would allow Mayor Frank L. Rizzo to seek a third term in office. Activist Milton Street pointed to Council President Schwartz, shouting his objections when Frissell was removed from the hearings.

PUBLISHED TUESDAY, JULY 25, 1978

Anna Ranieri of Rhawnhurst wearing a bumper sticker on her head calling for four more years of Rizzo, attends the City Council meeting whose agenda called for testimony on an amendment to the charter that would allow Philadelphia Mayor Frank L. Rizzo to seek a third term in office.

SUNDAY, APRIL 18, 1976

Former Philadelphia Mayor Joseph S. Clark (right) became the first city voter to sign a petition to recall Mayor Frank L. Rizzo. He told a crowd gathered on Independence Mall for the signing, "It's time to throw the rascal out." Clark told the approximately 200 spectators at the mid-morning event that Rizzo was guilty of "misfeasance and malfeasance in office," a remark that prompted a lone heckler to shout: "You never did nothin' wrong when you was in office, Clark?" The coalition of political and community groups must collect 145,488 signatures within 60 days. If the proper number of signatures is obtained, and if the mayor refuses to leave office voluntarily, the issue will be put on a ballot next fall.
UPDATE: Mayor Frank L. Rizzo will not have to face a recall referendum on whether he should be removed from office, the State Supreme Court ruled September 30, 1976.

PUBLISHED WEDNESDAY, SEPTEMBER 3, 1986

Three wounded Afghanistan guerrillas stepped off a military hospital jet at the Overseas Terminal, Philadelphia International Airport, to an emotional welcome from several dozen members of the local Afghan community. A Soviet flag supplied by Dr. Sayed Assadullah Ebady (with white beard) is stomped by a member of the local Afghan community, Mohammad Nader Shahalemi (left), and by one of the wounded guerrillas, Mohammed Nazir.
UPDATE: In accord with an agreement mediated by the United Nations and signed in Geneva on April 14, 1989, the USSR began withdrawing its troops from Afghanistan on May 15, 1989.

PUBLISHED WEDNESDAY, MARCH 16, 1977

Construction workers raise their placards as Philadelphia Finance Director Lennox L. Moak (foreground) waits to speak for the Center City Commuter Tunnel, the subject of some heated debate in the City Council chamber as people for or against the tunnel testified before the Council's committee on finance. The committee is expected to approve the $300 million project and to recommend approval to the full council. Nearly 300 persons crowded into the chamber to express their views.

UPDATE: On November 12, 1984, the $330 million Center City Commuter Tunnel was officially opened six years after construction began. The 1.7-mile tunnel linked the old Reading Railroad and Pennsylvania Railroad commuter lines into a unified 490-mile network that federal officials said was the only fully integrated regional rail system in the country.

THURSDAY, FEBRUARY 26, 1976

Placards protesting the Rizzo administration's plan to close Philadelphia General Hospital (PGH) are stacked overlooking the hospital in preparation for a demonstration by city employees and community residents. The rally was staged by labor, religious and civil rights groups, including Locals 1199 and 488 of the Hospital Workers Union, the NAACP, and District Councils 33 and 47 of the American Federation of State, County and Municipal Employees.

UPDATE: Philadelphia General Hospital closed its doors June 17, 1977.

PUBLISHED SUNDAY, JULY 11, 1976

Attending the Bicentennial Day celebration at Independence Hall are (from left), His Eminence John Cardinal Krol, President Gerald R. Ford and Philadelphia Mayor Frank L. Rizzo. Convoyed by a fleet of five helicopters from Valley Forge, President Ford called it the site where "the vein of iron in our national character was forged."

41

PUBLISHED SATURDAY, OCTOBER 21, 1972

President Richard M. Nixon and Philadelphia Mayor Frank L. Rizzo leave Independence Hall after Mr. Nixon signed into law on Friday a five-year, $30.2 billion dollar revenue-sharing program he said would usher in "a new American Revolution." Mr. Nixon told a group that revenue-sharing shows what the nation is capable of when we "act not as Democrats, Republicans or partisans, but as Americans."

PUBLISHED SATURDAY, JUNE 24, 1967

Rushing from his helicopter at the Boeing Flight Test Center Terminal after the summit talk with Soviet Premier Alexei Kosygin at Glassboro, N.J., President Lyndon B. Johnson shakes hands with Secretary of Defense Robert S. McNamara. The summit took place at the Holly Bush home of Glassboro State College President Thomas E. Robinson.
UPDATE: In 1997, Glassboro State College achieved university status and was renamed Rowen University after its benefactor, Henry Rowen.

PUBLISHED SUNDAY, JULY 11, 1976

During the Bicentennial Day celebration the Presidential Seal fell from the lectern at Independence Hall in the middle of President Gerald R. Ford's speech and was hastily tacked back into place by a Secret Service man. "Are the institutions under which we live working the way they should? Are the foundations laid in 1776 and 1789 still strong enough and sound enough to resist the tremors of our times?" he asked.

MONDAY, OCTOBER 6, 1980

With wife Nancy, Presidential candidate Ronald Reagan gives his supporters a thumbs-up smile while campaigning at the Cherry Hill Mall in New Jersey.
UPDATE: Voters repudiated the leadership of President Jimmy Carter November 4, 1980 and elected Ronald Reagan 40th President of the United States.

PUBLISHED FRIDAY, OCTOBER 31, 1980

President Jimmy Carter shakes hands with supporters after he told an audience of 100 Polish-Americans at Pilsudski Hall in Port Richmond that the Democratic Party was the party of human rights, religious tolerance and social progress.
UPDATE: Voters in all regions of the country resoundingly repudiated the leadership of President Jimmy Carter Tuesday, November 4, 1980 and elected Ronald Reagan 40th President of the United States.

PUBLISHED TUESDAY, AUGUST 18, 1981

Veterans and their spouses and friends gather at the Civic Center in Philadelphia to see Vice President George Bush don a Veterans of Foreign Wars cap during his address on the defense budget at the VFW convention.

43

PUBLISHED MONDAY, JANUARY 10, 1972

Speaking before a breakfast meeting of 1,200 Masons and their wives at the Scottish Temple in Collingswood, N.J., Vice President Spiro T. Agnew predicted that "an estimated 2.1 million new jobs" will be created in 1972 bringing the number of Americans holding jobs to a record 82 million, and the brightest prospects for peace that we have seen in many years. Behind the Vice President is the Cross of the Scottish Rite Temple.

PUBLISHED WEDNESDAY, SEPTEMBER 1, 1976

Secretary of State Henry A. Kissinger, who spoke to more than 1,000 persons attending the 12th annual convocation of Opportunities Industrialization Centers at Convention Hall, said the United States' diplomatic relationship with South Africa is based on the premise that it will move to end apartheid "within a reasonable period of time." Kissinger confers with the Rev. Leon Sullivan, founder and chairman of Opportunities Industrialization Centers.

PUBLISHED SATURDAY, APRIL 5, 1980

Senator Edward M. Kennedy ended a three-day swing through Pennsylvania after a morning of campaigning in Philadelphia. He charged that President Carter's proposed budget cuts would hurt the nation's big cities. "The budget cuts will work enormous hardships on the people," Kennedy said in an interview at *The Philadelphia Inquirer*.

FRIDAY, FEBRUARY 24, 1967

Senator Robert F. Kennedy arrives at the Bellevue Stratford Hotel in Philadelphia where he spoke at the 20th annual Roosevelt Day Dinner of the Southeastern Pennsylvania Chapter of Americans for Democratic Action. The New York Democrat said that the Nation cannot afford to ignore youth's questioning of the "basic premises" of the Vietnam war and must try to understand why they are "estranged" from today's world.

PUBLISHED MONDAY, AUGUST 2, 1965

Dr. Martin Luther King Jr. arrived at Philadelphia International Airport where a crowd of about 300 persons welcomed his arrival. Dr. King planned to visit Girard College, Philadephia's racial hot spot, during his two-day visit.

SATURDAY, SEPTEMBER 5, 1970

Black Panther chieftain Huey P. Newton (center) is surrounded by admirers at Philadelphia International Airport after his arrival to attend the Revolutionary Peoples Constitutional Convention, sponsored by the Black Panthers at Temple University. They were greeted by chants of "Power to the people."

PUBLISHED MONDAY, OCTOBER 28, 1968

Crowd jams Progress Plaza for the dedication of the Negro-owned facility at Broad and Oxford Streets in Philadelphia. In the foreground is the Rev. Leon Sullivan, innovator of the project. With him on the podium is the Very Rev. Thomas S. Logan Sr., (top hat) most worshipful grand master of Prince Hall Masons, Pennsylvania. "What you see before you today grew out of 200 members of my Zion Baptist Church six years ago," said Rev. Sullivan. What the 10,000 persons saw was a block of 16 stores, a spacious parking area and a sense of fulfillment by the Negro community that participated in the commercial enterprise.

PUBLISHED SUNDAY, JUNE 18, 1967

Philadelphia Mayor James H. J. Tate listens as the former Israeli Minister of Foreign Affairs, Golda Meir, at an "Action Rally for Israel" spurred pledges of more than $2.5 million in bonds for Israel. About 5,000 persons attended the rally at Convention Hall.

The Rev. Jesse Jackson speaks with a group at the Casimir Pulaski Pier Park. He is urging longshoremen and Teamsters to refuse to unload ships from South Africa. Jackson, who was in Philadelphia for a series of weekend events, urges people who have been protesting apartheid outside consulate buildings to move their picket lines to shipyards across America. "The battle ground must shift from the consulate to the shipyards."
UPDATE: President Clinton appointed civil rights leader Jesse Jackson as a roving ambassador in Africa. The announcement was made during a presidential visit to Philadelphia.

PUBLISHED FRIDAY, JUNE 24, 1977

Italian Senate President Amintore Fanfani (right) and John Cardinal Krol listen to Philadelphia Mayor Frank L. Rizzo at Fanfani's home. Fanfani accepted Mayor Frank L. Rizzo's offer to have 10 Italian police officers come to Philadelphia to study police work. The offer came in a discussion with Fanfani on the subject of street crime and terrorism in Italy. The Mayor said the way to treat criminals was "spacco il capo." The phrase, freely translated, means "break their heads." Fanfani started the discussion of police tactics, and the Mayor warmed to the occasion. Philadelphia's John Cardinal Krol served as translator. The Mayor previously attended the canonization of John Nepomucene Neumann, fourth bishop of Philadelphia.

PUBLISHED TUESDAY, OCTOBER 23, 1984

Walter F. Mondale, Democratic candidate for President (right) amid the crowd at JFK Plaza, shakes hands with actor Tony Randall who warmed up the crowd in Center City Philadelphia before the candidate's arrival. City Commissioner Margaret Tartaglione and District Attorney Edward Rendell are behind (centered) and Mrs. Mondale to the right of the candidate.

UPDATE: Ronald Wilson Reagan, the 40th President of the United States, won a landslide victory November 6, 1984 over his Democratic challenger, former Vice President Walter F. Mondale.

THURSDAY, NOVEMBER 1, 1984

Reminding women and Italian-Americans that she is one of their own, Democratic vice presidential candidate Geraldine A. Ferraro made her last pre-election stop in Philadelphia, campaigning for the women's and ethnic votes that Democrats hope will be especially drawn by her candidacy. Ferraro reminded people that "I am the first Italian-American to ever run for national office in this country."
UPDATE: Democratic challenger, former Vice President Walter F. Mondale, told a cheering crowd of supporters at the Civic Center in St. Paul, Minn. that he had telephoned President Ronald Reagan with his congratulations.

PUBLISHED TUESDAY, SEPTEMBER 11, 1984

Former Vice President and Democratic presidential nominee Walter F. Mondale with Congressman Thomas M. Foglietta while campaigning in Philadelphia at a construction site on 15th Street north of Chestnut Street. The Democratic presidential nominee, disclosed the broad details of a fiscal blueprint that he said would slash $177 billion from the expected 1989 budget deficit by boosting taxes and by slowing spending for military and some other programs, and challenged President Reagan to explain how he would trim deficits.
UPDATE: Ronald Wilson Reagan, the 40th President of the United States, won a landslide victory November 6, 1984 over his Democratic challenger, former Vice President Walter F. Mondale. Reagan, 73, received nearly three-fifths of the vote nationwide and recorded one of the most convincing presidential wins in American history, only narrowly failing to register the 50-state sweep that had been his campaign's goal in the closing days.
UPDATE: On Friday, September 5, 1997, President Bill Clinton nominated Rep. Thomas M. Foglietta (D., Pa.) to be U.S. ambassador to Italy. The nomination of the Democrat from South Philadelphia was unanimously approved on Tuesday, October 21, 1997 by the U.S. Senate. The grandson of Italian immigrants and nine-term congressman, Foglietta, 68, will be the first Philadelphian to be an ambassador since Walter H. Annenberg finished a six-year stint as envoy to Britain in 1974.

WEDNESDAY, NOVEMBER 5, 1986

Philadelphia Councilwoman Joan Specter laughs as her husband U.S. Senator Arlen Specter (R-Pa.) tries to keep his umbrella open after visiting the 34th Division in the 21st Ward. Specter, 56, officially claimed victory over his Democratic challenger, Rep. Bob Edgar.

UPDATE: On Friday, February 7, 1978, U.S. Senator Arlen Specter officially began another campaign, announcing that he is seeking a fourth six-year term in the Senate. No Pennsylvania senator has ever been elected four times. On November 7, 1995, Joan Specter narrowly lost re-election to an at-large City Council seat.

PUBLISHED TUESDAY, JUNE 21, 1983

Former Philadelphia Mayor Frank L. Rizzo, making his first public appearance since the night he lost the Democratic mayoral primary, endorsed the man who defeated him, W. Wilson Goode. With the former managing director at his side during a news conference at the Bellevue Stratford, Rizzo said he believed that Goode would be the next mayor of Philadelphia "with or without my endorsement. I ask those who would follow me to follow my advice instead," he said, "and vote for Wilson Goode in November."

SATURDAY, MAY 14, 1983

Philadelphia Democratic mayoral candidate Frank L. Rizzo (left) and Republican mayoral candidate John Egan greeted each other during the course of their campaign as they toured South Philadelphia's Italian Market. Egan, a Democrat and chairman of the Philadelphia Stock Exchange, became the first announced Republican candidate for mayor.
UPDATE: W. Wilson Goode was elected mayor of Philadelphia Tuesday, November 8, 1983, easily defeating his two rivals to become the city's first black chief executive in its 301-year history. With 99 percent of the vote counted, Democrat Goode led Republican John Egan by a 3-2 ratio, while independent candidate Thomas Leonard trailed far behind.

PUBLISHED TUESDAY, JANUARY 10, 1978

PUBLISHED SATURDAY, OCTOBER 31, 1970

Pledging to reform a state government that he said was a "national laughing stock," former State Auditor General Robert P. Casey announced his candidacy for the Democratic nomination for governor of Pennsylvania. Casey and family at the news conference (from left) Patrick, Margaret, Mary Ellen, Robert, Casey's wife Ellen, Chris, Kate, Erin and Matthew. Casey, 46, who ran for governor in 1966 and 1970 lost both times in the Democratic primary to Gov. Milton J. Shapp.
UPDATE: Democrat Pete F. Flaherty and Republican Richard L. Thornburgh, swept to victory, May 16, 1978 in their parties' respective primaries for the Pennsylvania gubernatorial nomination.
UPDATE: Democratic gubernatorial candidate Robert P. Casey, a man who had lost three times in his bid to become governor of Pennsylvania, won on his fourth try November 4, 1986, narrowly defeating Lieutenant Governor William W. Scranton 3d, his Republican rival.

Milton H. Shapp, Democratic candidate for governor of Pennsylvania, ignores his GOP opponent, Lt. Governor Raymond J. Broderick's handshake, after the program of the local chapter of the Sigma Delta Chi journalism fraternity dinner meeting at the Holiday Inn in Philadelphia. Each was arguing over the role Shapp played in the Democratic National Convention in Chicago in 1968
UPDATE: Shapp was elected governor of Pennsylvania November 3, 1970, in an unexpected Democratic sweep which captured both houses of the state Legislature for the first time in 32 years.
UPDATE: Milton J. Shapp, the millionaire businessman turned activist governor who gave Pennsylvania both the state lottery and the state income tax, died Thursday, November 24, 1994 at age 82. First elected in 1970, he was the first incumbent permitted under the new state constitution of 1968 to seek a second term. He was re-elected in 1974.

PUBLISHED TUESDAY, JANUARY 5, 1988

Ready to start his next four years, Philadelphia Mayor W. Wilson Goode waves to the audience of 2,000 people at the Academy of Music after Judge Tama Clark (behind him) administered the oath. Standing next to the mayor are Cardinal John Krol, Senator Arlen Specter and former Mayor William J. Green (right).

PUBLISHED SUNDAY, FEBRUARY 7, 1965

Supporters carry Cecil B. Moore after Moore's re-election as president of the
Philadelphia branch of the National Association for the Advancement of Colored People.
Moore defeated the Rev. Henry H. Nichols in a heated campaign.
UPDATE: Cecil B. Moore, 63, civil-rights activist, politician and lawyer died February
13, 1979. Moore's career in Philadelphia made him one of the most controversial black
leaders in the nation.

PUBLISHED TUESDAY, JANUARY 7, 1986

Outgoing District Attorney Edward G. Rendell (left) and Ronald D.
Castille, upon becoming Philadelphia's 31st district attorney,
renewed his promise to create a special investigations unit to
vigorously prosecute municipal and police corruption.
UPDATE: On Tuesday, November 2, 1993, Republican Ronald D.
Castille, 49, narrowly defeated his Democratic opponent,
Philadelphia Common Pleas Court Judge Russell M. Nigro, 47, in the
race for Pennsylvania Supreme Court Justice.
UPDATE: In 1991, Democrat Edward G. Rendell won the mayoralty
in a landslide over John Egan, who had been picked by the GOP
following Frank L. Rizzo's death. Rendell became the city's first
Jewish mayor.

PUBLISHED FRIDAY, JUNE 20, 1980

George X. Schwartz shakes hands with
Joseph E. Coleman, who as president pro
tempore succeeds him as head of the City
Council. Philadelphia City Council closed
ranks and unanimously elected
Councilman Joseph E. Coleman as its
president pro tempore. Coleman, 57, the
first black to head the council, succeeds
George X. Schwartz, who has resigned the
post because of his indictment in the
Abscam investigation.
UPDATE: Schwartz was sentenced
January 31, 1983, for conspiring to extort
money from undercover agents during the
Abscam investigation.

PUBLISHED FRIDAY, NOVEMBER 30, 1984

City Council's newest member, Angel L. Ortiz, displays figures of two roosters fighting, a Puerto Rican
tradition, a gift given to him at his swearing-in. Ortiz, accompanied by his wife, Lydia Hernandez
(right), is Council's first Puerto Rican councilman. The figures were presented by Brenda Rivera (left),
who sang with her father, Joaquin.

PUBLISHED SATURDAY, NOVEMBER 8, 1980

A knife in his hand, James Willis stands face to face with armed Philadelphia police officers at 28th and Girard Avenue. The confrontation occurred after Willis, 38, killed construction worker Walter Starks, 44, for no apparent reason. After a two-hour standoff, police hemmed Willis in, asking him to surrender. Using water guns, police finally knocked the 6-foot, 277-pound Willis to the pavement. Willis continued to struggle and to wield the knife as police tried to control him. Willis died at St. Joseph's Hospital of what a city examiner said was asphyxiation caused by a collapsed chest.

PUBLISHED TUESDAY, MARCH 27, 1973

PUBLISHED SATURDAY, JANUARY 10, 1987

Lawrence Bufalino (left) with uncle Russell Bufalino, 69-year-old reputed head of the five organized crime families operating in Pennsylvania who had been scheduled to be deported Monday, March 26 following an unsuccessful 16-year legal battle against the order. But last minute red tape between the U.S. Government and the Italian Consulate meant that Russell Bufalino, of Kingston, Pa., would not become Russell Bufalino, of Montedoro, Sicily for at least two more days.

UPDATE: Reputed Pennsylvania crime boss Russell Bufalino, 91, died Friday, February 25, 1994. James Kanavy, an agent with the Pennsylvania Crime Commission since 1973, said Mr. Bufalino's crime family was "one of the most powerful La Cosa Nostra families in the U.S. from the 1940's to the 1970's." Mr. Bufalino was born in Sicily, Italy. The U.S. Immigration and Naturalization Service unsuccessfully tried to deport him. When his appeals were exhausted in 1973, the Italian Foreign Ministry refused to issue a travel document for him, effectively blocking his deportation.

Reputed organized crime boss Nicodemo "Little Nicky" Scarfo approved and monitored a plan by Philadelphia City Councilman Leland M. Beloff, Beloff's top aide and an admitted mob figure to extort $1 million from Center City developer Willard G. Rouse 3d, according to a federal indictment made public Friday, January 9. The indictment portrayed Scarfo as a mobster who tried to spread the influence of organized crime into the city's legislative process through Beloff and the councilman's aide and longtime confidant, Robert Rego. En route to Philadelphia, Scarfo arrives for a hearing at federal court in Camden, New Jersey.

UPDATE: Nicodemo Scarfo's last hope of living long enough to get out of prison was extinguished May 2, 1990 when a Common Pleas Court judge sentenced him to life in prison plus at least six more years, to be served after the Philadelphia mob boss completes two federal prison terms amounting to 69 years. Scarfo and seven others were sentenced May 2, 1990 for the gangland killing of Frank "Frankie Flowers" D'Alfonso.

PUBLISHED FRIDAY, NOVEMBER 2, 1979

Reputed crime boss Angelo Bruno arriving at the courthouse in Trenton, N.J., risked a contempt-of-court charge and a return to jail when he twice refused to answer questions from the State Commission of Investigation about organized crime in the South Jersey-Philadelphia area.
UPDATE: Angelo Bruno, the leader of organized crime in Philadelphia for at least two decades, died Friday, March 21, 1980. The 69-year-old Bruno was shot to death at 9:50 p.m. in gang-execution style as he sat in his car in front of his South Philadelphia home.

PUBLISHED THURSDAY, APRIL 9, 1987

Gary Michael Heidnik, accused of murdering two women and raping and torturing four others held captive in a makeshift dungeon in the basement of his home at North Marshall street in the city's Franklinville section, is escorted to a sheriff's van outside City Hall in Philadelphia after his preliminary hearing was postponed.
UPDATE: A jury on July 2, 1988 sentenced Gary Michael Heidnik to death for the 1987 murders of Sandra Lindsay and Deborah Johnson Dudley, two of six women whom Heidnik held captive, chained and tortured in his basement. On March 2, 1989, Gary Michael Heidnick was sentenced to two death penalties and a prison term of up to 320 years by Common Pleas Court Judge Lynne M. Abraham. Scheduled to get a lethal injection, Heidnik, 45, was just a few hours from death at Rockview State Prison, April 19, 1997, when a ruling by the U.S. Supreme Court gave the torturer-murderer a second reprieve. On April 20, 1997, Heidnik was granted a stay of execution—for the present— by the Pennsylvania Supreme Court, seven hours before his death warrant expired.

PUBLISHED SATURDAY, JULY 3, 1982

Outside City Hall Courtroom 253, reactions to the jury's verdict range from shock to gratitude, after Mumia Abu-Jamal, 28, a former radio news reporter of some renown in Philadelphia, was found guilty yesterday of murdering Philadelphia police officer Daniel Faulkner on December 9 in Center City. The jury returned the first-degree murder verdict after deliberating five hours.

UPDATE: Mumia Abu-Jamal was sentenced to death July 3, 1982 for murdering Philadelphia police officer Daniel Faulkner. "I'd just like to thank the jury for being so courageous," said Maureen Faulkner, the officer's widow. "At least I'll be able to sleep again at night. But nothing— not the conviction or the penalty—will bring back my Danny."

PUBLISHED SATURDAY, JANUARY 30, 1965

Detective Lt. Michael Rotman (left) escorts Frank (The Hatchet) Phelan to Room 560 in City Hall, where the star witness in the Jack Lopinson murder trial will sleep. Phelan admitted he shot Lopinson's wife, Judy, 25, and his business associate Joseph (Joe Flowers) Malito in cold blood and returned several minutes later to deliver the coups de grace to each of the victims.

About 4 a.m. on the morning of June 19, 1964, Jack Lopinson called police to Dante's restaurant, 1809 Chestnut Street. Lopinson's wife Judy had been shot to death and one of the restaurant's owners, Joseph Malito, also had been killed. Jack Lopinson, a co-owner of the restaurant, had been shot in the leg. Lopinson, 27, told detectives that his wife had been in the basement office of the restaurant where Malito, 52, was counting the day's receipts about 3:30 a.m. Lopinson said he had been sitting at the bar upstairs when he heard shots. Two robbers emerged from the basement, each carrying a revolver. Lopinson fired but missed the intruders. The robbers fired back, hitting him in the leg and fled. When a medical examiner's inquest was held in mid-July 1964, an acquaintance of Lopinson's testified that Lopinson had spoken of wanting to "get rid of" his wife and boasted of knowing a hit man who could do the job. Lopinson, when called to testify, took the Fifth Amendment against self-incrimination. Lopinson was indicted on murder charges. Frank Phelan testified that he had killed Judy Lopinson and Joe Malito at Jack Lopinson's behest, then had shot Lopinson in the leg to make it look like a robbery. He said he had been paid $10,000. Phelan pleaded guilty to the killings and was sentenced to life in prison. Lopinson was convicted and sentenced to death in the electric chair. The sentence was commuted to life in prison in 1972.

PUBLISHED SATURDAY, JULY 29, 1978

Shortly after pleading innocent to federal racketeering and income tax evasion charges, Louis Vignola (left), president judge of the Philadelphia Traffic Court, leaves the federal building with attorney Thomas Bergstrom.

UPDATE: Former Traffic Court President Judge Louis Vignola was sentenced to serve two years at Allenwood Federal Prison for racketeering, and was fined $10,000 by Chief U.S. District Judge Joseph S. Lord 3rd in November 1978 for taking $32,000 in bribes from writ servers in exchange for giving them Traffic Court work.

PUBLISHED TUESDAY, FEBRUARY 4, 1986

After surrendering, Center City jeweler Ron Perlstein is taken from the district attorney's office for arraignment at the Police Administration Building. Perlstein, 34, turned himself in. He is charged with intentionally misrepresenting the weight, color and clarity of gems sold at this store, 801 Sansom Street in Philadelphia, during a four-year period.
UPDATE: Ron Perlstein was sentenced June 17, 1986 to four years probation and ordered to make restitution to more than 600 customers after pleading no contest to charges that he deceived them about the quality of their diamonds.

PUBLISHED SATURDAY, OCTOBER 10, 1987

Going to prison, former Philadelphia Register of Wills Robert W. Costigan is escorted to City Hall jail by a sheriff's deputy. After nearly five years of appeals, he began a two-to-five year sentence yesterday for the theft of thousands of dollars in cash and jewelry from the estate of a reputed mob figure, Chelsais "Steve" Booras. Booras was shot to death May 27, 1981, in the Meletis Restaurant on Eighth Street near Catherine Street. Costigan was convicted December 4, 1982 of conspiring with Booras' brother, John, to conceal more than $250,000 in cash and about $20,000 worth of jewelry from Booras' son. Costigan had acted as the estate's attorney.

PUBLISHED WEDNESDAY, SEPTEMBER 6, 1978

Jay C. Smith shields his face as he leaves a Paoli, Pa. hearing. Smith, convicted with William S. Bradfield for the 1979 murders of Upper Merion school teacher Susan Reinert and her two children, spent 6 years on death row. The Pennsylvania Supreme Court, however, threw out Smith's conviction on September 18, 1992, saying that the state had engaged in conduct during the trial so improper that Smith should not be retried for the crimes. Smith has always claimed his innocence. Bradfield, serving three consecutive life sentences, died Friday, January 16, 1998, in his cell at Graterford State Prison.

PUBLISHED SATURDAY, JANUARY 26, 1985

Dr. Joseph Melnick leaves a courtroom in City Hall after his hearing is recessed for lunch. Problems in the prosecution of Dr. Joseph Melnick, charged with murder and abortion-law violations, arose during a preliminary hearing when a nurse backed away from previous statements she had made to police and refused to testify that the doctor had acted improperly. UPDATE: A remorseful Dr. Joseph Melnick, on December 19, 1989 was sentenced to 300 hours of community service and three years probation on his conviction for baby-killing under the state's abortion control law. But, to the delight of his attorney and family, the 66-year-old Overbrook gynecologist was neither sentenced to a prison term nor fined.

PUBLISHED FRIDAY, APRIL 8, 1988

Former Philadelphia Common Pleas Court Judge Herbert R. Cain Jr. (center), is escorted by his attorney Morris Paul Baran (left), and his son, Randy, after U.S. District Judge Edmund V. Ludwig sentenced Cain to three years in prison, saying that Cain's acceptance of a payoff had threatened "everything our judicial system is supposed to stand for." In addition to the prison term, Ludwig ordered Cain to pay a $5,000 fine and $1,500 in restitution.

PUBLISHED FRIDAY, NOVEMBER 7, 1986

Philadelphia Councilman Leland M. Beloff and his wife Diane leaving Federal Court after they entered not-guilty pleas during arraignment to extortion and fraud counts.

UPDATE: Beloff was convicted July 2, 1987 of plotting with mob boss Nicodemo Scarfo to extort $1 million from developer Willard G. Rouse. The then-councilman also pleaded guilty to forging absentee ballots. He served nearly six years as a federal prisoner. Diane Beloff was placed on two years' probation.

PUBLISHED THURSDAY, FEBRUARY 16, 1978

Former State Senator Henry J. (Buddy) Cianfrani, (left), leaving courtroom with two friends is followed by a crowd of reporters after Cianfrani was sentenced to five years in prison for bribery, racketeering and mail fraud. The jail sentence of Cianfrani, 54, a South Philadelphia Democrat who was, until last year, one of the most powerful men in state government, is to be followed by five years of probation.

UPDATE: After Cianfrani served 27 months at Allenwood Federal Penitentiary and eight years of semipolitical exile, he emerged once again in 1988 as a Democratic ward leader where he started in 1955.

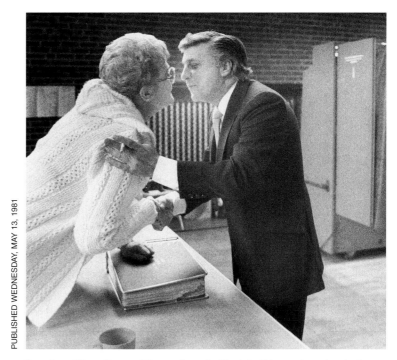

PUBLISHED WEDNESDAY, MAY 13, 1981

Camden, New Jersey Mayor Angelo Errichetti greets vote clerk Betty Santanello at the Bonsall School during Mayoral election day. Convicted of bribery and conspiracy in the federal government's Abscam investigation in the summer of 1980, Errichetti was sentenced August 13, 1981, to six years in prison and fined $40,000. The former mayor must serve at least two years before he is eligible for parole. Errichetti had yielded his Camden mayoral seat in December, 1980, declining to run for re-election.

PUBLISHED SATURDAY, FEBRUARY 27, 1982

Jubilant supporters shower Philadelphia city councilman Harry P. Jannotti with hugs and kisses after the City Council voted 13-2, heeding the advice of City Solicitor Alan J. Davis not to bar him from council meetings until the day after Jannotti is sentenced for his Abscam conviction on bribery and conspiracy charges.
UPDATE: Former Councilman Harry P. Jannotti was sentenced to prison Monday, January 31, 1983 for conspiring to extort money from undercover FBI agents during the Abscam investigation. U.S. District Judge John P. Fullam sentenced Jannotti, 58, to six months in prison and fined him $2,000.

PUBLISHED WEDNESDAY, JANUARY 6, 1988

Former New Jersey State Senator David Friedland arrives at the U.S. Courthouse in Camden, N.J. for arraignment. Friedland pleaded not guilty to a 90-count indictment charging him with mail fraud and racketeering in connection with a plan to skim millions from the pension fund of Local 701 of the Teamsters in New Brunswick. UPDATE: In a Camden courtroom, former New Jersey State Senator David Friedland was sentenced December 2, 1988 to 15 years in prison. Friedland received the sentence for defrauding the pension fund of North Brunswick Teamsters Local 701. In 1980, a judge had sentenced Friedland to seven years for defrauding the same fund. The two sentences will run concurrently.

PUBLISHED SATURDAY, JANUARY 17, 1987

Dr. Martin Spector leaves court with his wife, Annette, after the Philadelphia physician and three morgue workers were ordered held for trial on charges that Spector conspired with them to buy and resell body parts, heads, arms, and ear bones that had been stolen from three city hospitals. Spector, 70, an ear, nose and throat specialist, faces charges of conspiracy, theft, receiving stolen property and abuse of corpse, all criminal offenses, and a violation of the state health code, which prohibits interstate transportation of body parts.
UPDATE: On October 26, 1988, Common Pleas Judge Mark I. Bernstein fined Dr. Martin Spector $35,000 - the maximum allowable. He also ordered Spector to complete 1,600 hours of community service work at a prison clinic and forbade him to charge for professional services until he had completed the first 300 hours of volunteer work.

PUBLISHED MONDAY, MAY 21, 1973

PUBLISHED MONDAY, AUGUST 23, 1971

Defendants (from left) Lianne Moccia, Rosemary Reilly, Ann Dunham, Margaret Inness and Sarah Tosi are escorted by U.S. Marshals from the U.S. Courthouse in Camden, N.J. after their arraignment on charges of attempting to steal and destroy draft records at the Selective Service office in Camden.
UPDATE: Seventeen members of the "Camden 28" were acquitted May 20, 1973 on charges of breaking into the Selective Service office here on August 21, 1971 and destroying draft records. The acquittals, announced by jury foreman James Lomax after three days of deliberations, represented the first complete legal victory for the antiwar movement in a series of trials stretching over the last five years.

A youth cries in exultation outside the Federal Courthouse in Camden, New Jersey after 17 members of the "Camden 28" were acquitted Sunday on charges of breaking into the Selective Service office here on August 21, 1971, and destroying draft records.

PUBLISHED TUESDAY, FEBRUARY 24, 1981

Former U.S. Attorney General Ramsey Clark, flanked by protesters as he leaves the Montgomery County Courthouse in Norristown, Pa., where he and two other attorneys will act only as advisors during the trial of the eight defendants charged with burglary, criminal trespass, criminal conspiracy and related offenses in the break-in at the General Electric plant last September 9, in King of Prussia, Pa. The defendants have said that the incident was a protest against the arms race. Among the defendants are Daniel Berrigan, 59, of New York City and brother former priest Philip Berrigan, 57, of Baltimore, Md.

PUBLISHED TUESDAY, FEBRUARY 24, 1981

Montgomery County Common Pleas Court Judge Samuel W. Salus said he wanted to make it clear that the eight defendants before him were to be tried for allegedly breaking into and vandalizing a General Electric Company plant. The eight defendants are charged with burglary, criminal trespass, criminal conspiracy and related offenses in the break-in at the GE plant last September 9. They allegedly damaged a missile nose cone and poured blood on company documents. The defendants have said that the incident was a protest against the arms race. The defendants (from left) Jesuit priest Daniel Berrigan, 59, of New York City; former priest Philip Berrigan, 57, of Baltimore, Md.; Sister Ann Montgomery, 54, of New York City; John Schuchardt, 41, a Baltimore lawyer; Molly Rush, 45, of suburban Pittsburgh; Dean Hammer, 26, of New Haven, Conn.; Elmer Maas, 45, of New York City; The Rev. Carl Kabat, 47, of Baltimore, Md.; and attorney Charles A. Glackin.

UPDATE: The anti-war activist Berrigan brothers and the six other members of the "Plowshares Eight" were sentenced to prison July 28, 1981 for burglary in a break-in at a nuclear-missile components plant.

PUBLISHED WEDNESDAY, JUNE 10, 1987

Actress Brooke Shields, whose professional career began at the age of 11 months when she was chosen as the Ivory Soap baby, added another credential to her resume—she earned an honors degree from Princeton University. Wearing a traditional black mortarboard and gown, a smiling Brooke Shields led Princeton's class of 1987 in the commencement procession past photographers and camera crews from as far away as Japan. "I did it," Shields, 22, told reporters. "I've proven something to myself," Shields said. "I didn't expect to get honors, but I worked as hard as I could from day one."

71

PUBLISHED THURSDAY, JULY 19, 1984

Bob Hope and entertainer Ann Jillian sing for workers and USS Forrestal crew at the Philadelphia Naval Shipyard.

PUBLISHED THURSDAY, JULY 19, 1984

Bob Hope brought his jokes and songs to the Philadelphia Naval Shipyard during a half-hour visit to entertain the workers and crew of the aircraft carrier USS Forrestal, which since January has been undergoing a 28-month renovation. Hope, who with entertainer Ann Jillian is performing in the area, wanted to visit the crew of the carrier that saw action during the Suez Canal crisis and the Vietnam War. After a brief performance, Hope autographed hats for the crew of the carrier.

PUBLISHED TUESDAY, SEPTEMBER 14, 1971

Anyone who has seen the hit film "Carnal Knowledge" certainly has vivid recollections of the sad, tragic figure portrayed by Ann-Margaret. But then, on the other hand, anyone who has seen Ann-Margaret knows there is nothing sad or tragic about her figure. This was delightfully evident when Ann-Margaret strolled into the parlor of her suite at the Rickshaw Inn in Cherry Hill, N.J. Naturally, the lovely lady is pleased with the excited reception awarded her work in "Carnal Knowledge." "I'm overwhelmed," she conceded. "What can I say? I never expected it. But I have to be honest, it was the most difficult role I've ever had. It just drained me emotionally."

PUBLISHED THURSDAY, NOVEMBER 4, 1982

Back to Central High School, comedian Bill Cosby talks to young people after receiving his track and field and football letters and addressing the students. Cosby earned the letters as a member of Central's 206th class, which graduated in 1956, but had lost them. He was presented with the school's Barnwell Distinguished Service Award at a banquet at the Bellevue Stratford Hotel in Philadelphia.

PUBLISHED THURSDAY, NOVEMBER 23, 1978

Back on home turf, Sylvester Stallone strode Chestnut Street and his crew began filming "Rocky 2." Scene 33, Take 4 began with a "clap" at the J.E. Caldwell Co. at Chestnut and Juniper Streets. Stallone, a former Philadelphian, created a huge box-office success with his first film, "Rocky," which was made here; and, although reviewers criticized his latest effort, "Paradise Alley," fans turned out in numbers to watch the doings.

PUBLISHED FRIDAY, OCTOBER 8, 1965

Andy Warhol, most noted of the contemporary pop artists, poses with one of his 12 life-size pictures of Elvis Presley at the University of Pennsylvania. There were 52 pictures of the late actress Marilyn Monroe, 200 pictures of dollar bills, 66 of Jacqueline Kennedy and 210 pictures of coke bottles.
UPDATE: Andy Warhol died in a Manhattan hospital, February 22, 1987

PUBLISHED SATURDAY, JULY 15, 1967

PUBLISHED MONDAY, MAY 14, 1973

Surrounded by his "security guards," Frank Sinatra pulls away from Civic Center Convention Hall after his concert. Wife Mia is hidden behind Sinatra. As the performance broke, two dapper "associates" of the crooner were quietly insisting, "You will not get a picture of Sinatra." As Mia and husband came out, the two "associates" made sure no pictures would be taken...they stood in front of the photographer's camera, shielding the Sinatras. But the cameraman, not to be outdone in ingenuity, ducked to the side as the Sinatra car pulled away and made the shot, much to the chagrin of the "associates." Philadelphia Police Commissioner Frank L. Rizzo made it "clear" to the "associates" that not one finger would be laid on the photographer.
UPDATE: Frank Sinatra's marriage to Mia Farrow lasted two years.
UPDATE: Congress bestowed its highest award on Tuesday, April 29, 1997, on entertainer Frank Sinatra, awarding him a gold medal commemorating his six-decade career as a singer and an actor.
UPDATE: Francis Albert Sinatra, the 20th century's most celebrated saloon singer, died Thursday, May 14, 1998 in Los Angeles. Mr. Sinatra was 82.

Mrs. Frances Liberace was honored in Doylestown, Pa., as the Polish-American Mother of the Year. Mrs. Liberace, ill in Los Angeles with the London flu, was not present for the award, which was accepted in her behalf by her daughter Angie and son Wladziu Liberace, the noted showman and pianist. In a brief acceptance speech before a crowd of more than one thousand, Liberace noted that he had frequently told audiences what a wonderful mother he had and that now it was being acknowledged by the world at large. "I think," he said, referring to his affection for his mother, "it's practically legendary now." Mrs. Liberace is the third recipient of the annual award presented at The National Shrine of Our Lady of Czestochowa.
UPDATE: Entertainer Liberace, 67, died February 4, 1987 at his home in Palm Springs, California.

PUBLISHED MONDAY, FEBRUARY 28, 1966

Freddie Mason, 10, of Lansdale, Pa., (left) and Allan Cabal, 12, of Camden, N.J., members of the Police Athletic League, and David Kohn, chairman of the PAL board of directors, present entertainer Jimmy Durante with awards for his service to PAL. He was honored at a dinner at the Hotel Philadelphia. Police Captain Clarence J. Ferguson (rear) joins in.

UPDATE: Jimmy Durante, 87, the man with a million of 'em, died January 29, 1980. Durante closed each show with the wistful line, "Goodnight, Mrs. Calabash, wherever you are." He never revealed the identity of Mrs. Calabash, saying: "A fella's gotta have some secrets, don't he?"

UPDATE: Captain Clarence J. Ferguson, 75, died November 7, 1971. Captain Clarence J. (Fergy) Ferguson joined the Philadelphia police force on August 27, 1919, and in the following half-century, earned more commendations, citations and honors than any other man on the force.

PUBLISHED SUNDAY, MARCH 30, 1975

Actress Cybill Shepherd takes a stroll down Broad Street during her visit to Philadelphia. Cybill talks about her new movie, "At Long Last Love," a light musical romance in which she sings and dances for the first time, and about her role as Brooks Carter, the part of a young, beautiful and super-indulged rich kid, not unlike her role as the young, beautiful and super-indulged Jacy in "The Last Picture Show," her first movie.

WFIL-TV Bandstand moderator Dick Clark is set to tape interviews with some of his former regular dancers who appeared on his show. Michelle Leibowitz, 18, of Philadelphia is first in line to be interviewed.
UPDATE: A plaque honoring the Philadelphia TV dance show was unveiled August 5, 1997, at the old WFIL-TV studios, at 46th and Market Streets, during a celebration of the 40th anniversary of "American Bandstand." On August 5, 1957, Dick Clark, then 27, took the local dance show to the nationwide ABC network on weekday afternoons.

PUBLISHED SATURDAY, MARCH 19, 1983

It was a big day for Fabian, one of the rock stars of the late '50s and early '60s. He went back to his alma mater, George C. Thomas Junior High School, Ninth and Johnson Streets in Philadelphia, and was inducted into its Hall of Fame. With the singer (right), whose full name is Fabian Forte, is Joseph L. Pollock, school principal.

PUBLISHED TUESDAY, MARCH 8, 1983

A Brenner bash takes place on Ch. 6's "AM/Philadelphia" as David Brenner is paid a surprise visit by his parents, Lou and Estelle. The comedian, a city native, was here promoting his memoirs, "Soft Pretzels With Mustard."

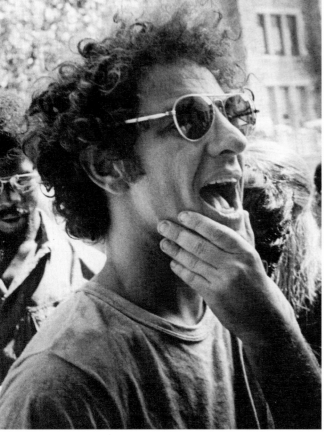

PUBLISHED SUNDAY, SEPTEMBER 6, 1970

Abbie Hoffman, "Chicago 7" figure, gesturing as he talks with newsmen during a convention at Temple University's McGonigle Hall where nearly 10,000 delegates and followers of the new left peacefully assembled in Philadelphia for the opening of the Revolutionary People's Constitutional Convention sponsored by the Black Panthers, and calling on all minorities in the country to become revolutionaries. UPDATE: Abbie Hoffman, 52, a '60s political activist, took his own life, Wednesday, April 12, 1989. Hoffman and others in the Chicago Seven were prosecuted for conspiracy to incite violence in the 1968 Democratic National Convention in Chicago.

PUBLISHED SUNDAY, JULY 8, 1973

John Carradine flew in from North Dakota, where he had acted, directed and designed scenery for a university production of "A Man For All Seasons." The 67-year-old actor's destination was New Hope, where he opened as Gramps in "On Borrowed Time" at the Bucks County Playhouse. UPDATE: John Carradine, 82, died November 27, 1988 in Milan, Italy. He appeared in, by his own estimate, about 500 films.

79

PUBLISHED MONDAY, JANUARY 22, 1968

Actress Helen Hayes receives the Philadelphia Art Alliance Award of Merit from Raymond S. Green, president of the organization, at the Art Alliance. The award is given "in recognition of outstanding creative work of high artistic merit." Helen Hayes smiled demurely as people stood in line at the Philadelphia Art Alliance to welcome her to the city.
UPDATE: Helen Hayes, 92, actress, stage, movies and television, died March 17, 1993.

SUNDAY, MARCH 7, 1976

Princess Grace of Monaco, the former Grace Kelly of Philadelphia, was among the 90 judges who awarded 48 major competitive prizes at a special preview of The Philadelphia Flower Show at the Civic Center, attended by more than 10,000 Horticultural Society members and their guests.
UPDATE: Grace Kelly, 52, the Philadelphia girl who first became a queen in Hollywood and then, in a real-life Cinderella story, became the princess of Monaco, died Tuesday, September 14, 1982 from injuries she suffered in a car crash.

PUBLISHED SUNDAY, OCTOBER 17, 1971

Maxie Furman is the provisional manager of the Troc Theater, the only burlesque action within 60 miles of Philadelphia. "Provisional" is important because, although he has been connected with the Troc for 15 years, Maxie still thinks of himself in terms of what he has been for 40 years. "People are under a misconception," he explains patiently. "I still work as an entertainer. I'm an actor. A year ago I did 25 weeks in Vegas." A loyal son of burlesque, Maxie, 60, holds the hand of this 100-year-old dying grande dame 14 hours a day, seven days a week at 10th and Arch Streets. Maxie is at his most serene and respectful when surrounded by reminders of better days, as he toasts old glories at the Show Bar adjacent to the Troc.

UPDATE: Max S. Furman, 73, who spent his life in burlesque, died Tuesday, February 19, 1985. Max managed the Troc during its waning years, providing Philadelphia's last showcase for G-string clad, bump-and-grind beauties and the baggy-pants comedians who provided the between-the-acts action.

PUBLISHED FRIDAY, OCTOBER 17, 1986

Erno Rubik the Hungarian inventor of Rubik's Cube, with his latest puzzle, Rubik's Magic. "It's like a mousetrap," Rubik said. "It looks easy, but then you get caught." Rubik, 42, is winding up a three-week promotional tour around the United States. He is happiest at home in Budapest, Hungary, thinking up new designs. "The biggest game for me is to make another one that does not exist yet," Rubik said.

PUBLISHED THURSDAY, FEBRUARY 4, 1982

James Hulse Dolsen, at 96 is still active in the communist movement in the United States. He lives in two rooms in Philadelphia, filled with the clutter of a lifetime dedicated to the party. Dolsen was there in the beginning. At the 1919 convention in Chicago when the Communist Labor Party split from the old Socialist Party, he chaired the committee to draft the new party's constitution.
UPDATE: A founder of the Communist Party U.S.A., James H. Dolsen, 103, for more than six decades worked to create a communist United States. It remained his mission until he died November 30, 1988.

PUBLISHED SATURDAY, NOVEMBER 20, 1976

Peering over glasses, Rosalynn Carter, wife of President-elect Jimmy Carter, attends a meeting on mental health at the Benjamin Franklin Hotel in Philadelphia. On November 19, she called for the establishment of a Presidential Commission on Mental Health and Mental Retardation. "This is one of the first things I want Jimmy to do," the President-elect's wife said, addressing the concluding session of the annual meeting of the Mental Health Association.

MONDAY, NOVEMBER 10, 1969

Muhammed Kenyatta was greeted by a Jewish Defense League picket line and an attentive audience at Main Line Reform Temple for a Black Manifesto discussion. The Black Economic Development Conference Leader had been invited by a group of the Wynnewood congregation to talk about the BED's demands for $500 million in "black reparations." His appearance prompted peaceful picketing by the JDL members who regarded his presence as a "desecration of the temple."

PUBLISHED MONDAY, FEBRUARY 14, 1966

James R. Hoffa (left) international president of the Teamsters Union, talks with John P. Greeley, Camden, N.J. Local 676 president, at a dinner honoring Greeley, held at the Armory in Woodbury, N.J.
UPDATE: Hoffa, powerful president of the International Brotherhood of Teamsters (1957-71), which he helped build into the world's largest labor union, was convicted of malfeasance in office and other charges in 1964 and entered prison in 1967, but had his thirteen-year prison sentence commuted by President Richard M. Nixon in 1971. Hoffa is believed to have been abducted near Detroit on July 30, 1975. He was declared "presumed dead" on December 8, 1982.

MONDAY, JANUARY 18, 1965

Capt. Eddie Rickenbacker, (left), American flying ace of the First World War, with Ruritan national president, Rev. Russell Burgess of Petersburg, West Virginia, attends the 35th Ruritan National Convention in Philadelphia.
UPDATE: Edward V. Rickenbacker died July 23, 1973. Known as "Captain Eddie," Rickenbacker earned the Congressional Medal of Honor for daredevil exploits as combat pilot and air squadron commander against German fighter planes in 1918.

PUBLISHED FRIDAY, OCTOBER 2, 1981

Harold Russell enjoys a cup of coffee as he talks about his work with the handicapped. "Not long ago," he said, "I was in an airport waiting for a flight, and I got to chatting with a woman sitting across from me. She kept glancing at my hooks, then quickly looked away. Finally she got up enough nerve to tell me about a film she had seen on late-night TV." What the woman told Harold Russell was that one of the characters was a young sailor who had lost both hands during World War II but, using prosthetic devices, had been able to overcome his handicap. "Try to see it," the woman said, "I'm sure you'd find it encouraging. It's called The Best Years of Our Lives." The woman may never know that she had been talking to the man who played the handless sailor, winning the 1946 Academy Award for Best Supporting Actor for his performance in what is widely considered to be one of the all-time great American films. Since the mid-1960s, Russell, 67, has been chairman of the President's Commission on Employment of the Handicapped.

85

Consumer Party Activist and third party candidate for Council At Large, Max Weiner, uses a bullhorn during a demonstration in front of the State Office Building at Broad and Spring Garden Streets, calling on insurance Commissioner Constance B. Foster to reject the insurance rate requests.
UPDATE: Max Weiner, 77, a city controller candidate who was best known as Philadelphia's tenacious advocate for the consumer, died October 22, 1989.

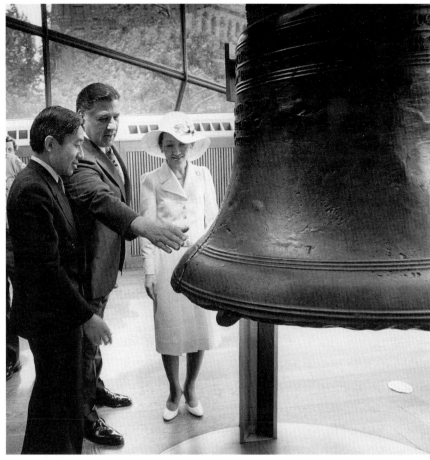

PUBLISHED TUESDAY, JUNE 27, 1978

Japan's Crown Prince Akihito, heir to the oldest throne in the world, checks out the Liberty Bell with Princess Michiko and Philadelphia Mayor Frank L. Rizzo. The Prince is the son of Emperor Hirohito and, according to legend, a direct descendant of the Sun Goddess.
UPDATE: Emperor Akihito formally ascended the throne of Japan, November 13, 1990 in the world's oldest royal line.

PUBLISHED MONDAY, MAY 6, 1974

Britain's Princess Margaret and her husband, Lord Snowdon, came to Philadelphia for receptions, a party and sightseeing at the Art Museum and at Independence Hall. Princess Margaret pauses and smiles for newsmen before entering her car as she leaves the Philadelphia Museum of Art.

PUBLISHED SUNDAY, JULY 12, 1970

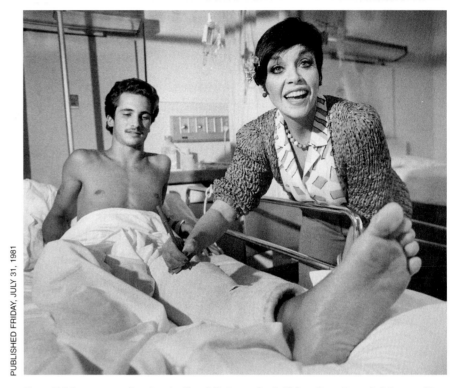

PUBLISHED FRIDAY, JULY 31, 1981

Jaye P. Morgan, enthusiastically obliging a bedridden fan, Joseph Marra, 19, of Philadelphia, during the singer's visit to Children's Hospital. She is appearing in the Carousel Café at Resorts International in Atlantic City.

Christine Jorgensen, in Philadelphia last week to talk about a new motion picture which bears her name. "The Christine Jorgensen Story," scoffed at the idea that a transsexual change such as hers would rate headlines today. "In fact, the kind of operation I had isn't even news anymore," Miss Jorgensen said. "It's done all the time and nobody pays any attention to it." But back in 1953 when the new Miss Jorgensen, at age 27, stepped off the plane from Denmark at New York's International Airport, she created a sensation in the press. Headlines screamed about the ex-Bronx GI George Jorgensen Jr., who wired: Dear Mom and Dad, I have become your daughter."
UPDATE: Christine Jorgensen, 62, a former soldier who in 1952 underwent the first publicized sex-change operation to be transformed into a woman, died May 3, 1989.

PUBLISHED THURSDAY, OCTOBER 5, 1978

Anne L. Armstrong (right), the only woman ever to serve as U.S. ambassador to Britain, came to the Benjamin Franklin Hotel in Philadelphia to address a World Affairs Council luncheon. During the reception, which preceded the luncheon, Mrs. Armstrong was greeted warmly by Walter H. Annenberg and his wife, Lee. Mr. Annenberg served as U.S. ambassador to Britain for 5 ½ years.

PUBLISHED SATURDAY, OCTOBER 8, 1966

Artist Andrew Wyeth (left) was awarded the Gold Medal by the Pennsylvania Academy of the Fine Arts on the eve of the opening of an exhibition of his works there. Frank T. Howard, (right), President of the Academy made the presentation. It is the 36th such medal given in the last 73 years.

PUBLISHED MONDAY, SEPTEMBER 10, 1979

Dr. C. Everett Koop, surgeon-in-chief at Children's Hospital in Philadelphia, told the audience at the Academy of Music, that abortion claims the lives of one million unborn babies a year in this country. The film-lecture series "Whatever happened to the Human Race?" came to Philadelphia beginning a 20-city tour of the United States. The film-lecture series was prepared and presented by Dr. C. Everett Koop, Dr. Francis A. Schaeffer, a fundamentalist theologian and philosopher, and Schaeffer's son, Franky Schaeffer 5th, a filmmaker who shot the five-part movie.
UPDATE: C. Everett Koop began his medical career as chief surgeon at Children's Hospital in Philadelphia in 1948 and practiced here until accepting President Ronald Reagan's offer to come to Washington as Surgeon General in 1981.

PUBLISHED WEDNESDAY, SEPTEMBER 23, 1981

Philadelphia Orchestra Maestro Eugene Ormandy (center) meets with new orchestra members (from left) Kazuo Tokita, piccolo, a Sapporo native who had played in Vancouver and with the CBC Chamber orchestra; David Cramer, associate principal flute, who had played in Montreal and Pittsburgh; Patrick Connolly, violist, who had played in Dallas, Mexico City and Pittsburgh; Charles G. Vernon, bass trombonist, who had played in Baltimore and San Francisco. UPDATE: Eugene Ormandy, 86, symphony conductor, was music director of the Philadelphia Orchestra for forty-four years, died March 12, 1985.

PUBLISHED MONDAY, SEPTEMBER 21, 1964

Dr. Eugene Ormandy, conductor of the Philadelphia Orchestra, and his wife, Gretel, stride between an honor guard of Cardinal Dougherty High School drum majorettes at International Airport. The couple and 85 musicians received a rousing reception after a triumphant 26-day transcontinental tour.

Jozsef Molnar and his 12-foot Swiss alpenhorn rehearses with the Philadelphia Orchestra under the watchful eye of Eugene Ormandy. Molnar arrived in Philadelphia this week accompanied by Jean Daetwyler, the Swiss composer of the concerto he plays in the weekend concerts. Molnar will stand at stage center as the first alpenhorn soloist in the orchestra's history.

PUBLISHED MONDAY, NOVEMBER 29, 1965

PUBLISHED TUESDAY, MAY 19, 1987

Camden's most important social event in decades began at 8:30 P.M., Sunday November 27, 1965 when the new Camden Symphony Orchestra performed for the first time at Philadelphia's Academy of Music. The 90-member orchestra, sponsored by Camden, is composed of leading musicians from Philadelphia, New York and South Jersey. Founder and conductor Ling Tung of the new orchestra, discusses the program for Sunday evening's premier performance with Camden Mayor Alfred R. Pierce and soloist for the evening, Metropolitan Opera soprano Anna Moffo. The Academy was chosen as the area's finest concert hall with hopes that some day, Camden may have its own culture center.

Riccardo Muti, who received an honorary doctorate at the University of Pennsylvania's 231st commencement ceremony, told 3,500 graduates, "a society that lacks openness and receptivity is a society in deep trouble. When receptive people hear Beethoven's Ninth Symphony, no matter where they are, they know they are in the presence of the great thought and a great feeling," the artistic director of the Philadelphia Orchestra said in a commencement address at Franklin Field.

UPDATE: Riccardo Muti stunned the Philadelphia Orchestra March 29, 1990 by announcing that he would step down as its music director at the end of August 1992. Muti kept the orchestra's members after their afternoon rehearsal in the Academy of Music to announce his decision.

PUBLISHED SUNDAY, FEBRUARY 22, 1976

The orchestra had turned into a brass band and was playing a march that sounded like the Fourth of July gone to heaven. The music was quick and sassy and full of verve. "Trumpets!" said Leonard Bernstein, attending a rehearsal at Town Hall in Philadelphia. "I go around knocking on wood," Bernstein says as he awaits the opening of his musical "1600 Pennsylvania Avenue"; things are going too well for this one." Past triumphs for his music on Broadway, "West Side Story," "Candide," "Wonderful Town," "On The Town" must count for something. His fame as a conductor and composer of symphonic music must add weight. But for the time being, Bernstein is a prisoner of the Broadway dictum that you're only as good as your last show. UPDATE: Leonard Bernstein, 72, the impassioned American maestro who thrilled the world with "On The Town" and West Side Story," his podium pirouettes and hundreds of recordings, died in his Manhattan apartment, October 14, 1990. Mr. Bernstein had announced his retirement from conducting on October 9. He led the orchestra on tours of South America, Europe and Asia, and on numerous national television appearances. He televised Young People's Concerts, and helped introduce the baby-boom generation to classical music and won 11 Emmy Awards.

PUBLISHED TUESDAY, APRIL 17, 1984

Trumpeter Wynton Marsalis (right) listens to Overbrook High School senior David Gaines, 18, onstage at the Philadelphia Community College. Marsalis, on the Academy of Music stage the night before, points out some technical details, some ways of thinking about high notes so they don't seem so high, and an image or two to suggest what the music means. He tells Gaines, "We trumpet players are always wondering if we're going to hit the right note." He adds, "It's like a wide receiver going downfield for an 80-yard bomb and wondering if he'll catch it." About 200 people came to Community College, many carrying instrument cases. They came on a chance they would hear Marsalis play or hear him encourage them to do what he has done.

PUBLISHED SATURDAY, JUNE 6, 1964

Phillies' fans line up outside Connie Mack Stadium at 21st and Lehigh Avenue as the largest crowd of the season fills the park to see the National League leaders meet the San Francisco Giants in the opener of a three-game series in front of 31,774 fans. The Giants beat the Phils in the 11th inning. Giants Orlando Cepeda's home run in the 8th ties the score and sets the stage for the 5-3 loss.
UPDATE: On October 1, 1970, Connie Mack Stadium, the oldest major league baseball park in the country, played host to the last of more than 6,000 baseball games. A new field, Veterans Stadium, was being readied at Broad Street and Pattison Avenue in South Philadelphia.

PUBLISHED SUNDAY, JULY 26, 1970

PUBLISHED MONDAY, SEPTEMBER 6, 1971

New York Mets first base coach Yogi Berra points, laughing, into the Phillies dugout during a game in which the Phils end an 8-game losing streak, 7-3.

Phillies' Bill Nicholson talks things over with A's Hall of Famer, Lefty Grove, before the start of Saturday evening's Old-Timers game at Connie Mack Stadium. Phillies beat the A's, 1-0.

UPDATE: Robert Moses (Lefty) Grove, 75, whose fastball won the 1920-30-31 American League pennants for the Philadelphia Athletics, died May 22, 1975. Grove struck out 2,266 and had a 3.06 earned-run average while gaining his place in the Hall of Fame with a 300-140 record for a phenomenal .682 winning percentage. He had eight 20-victory seasons, including a 31-4 record in 1931.

UPDATE: Bill Nicholson, 81, an outfielder with the 1950 National League champion Phillies whose forceful left-handed swing earned him the nickname "Swish," died Friday, March 8, 1996. Bill Nicholson twice led the National League in home runs and, as a member of the Phillies' "Whiz Kids," Mr. Nicholson was credited with helping get the team to the 1950 World Series.

PUBLISHED TUESDAY, JUNE 12, 1979

A young PAL, Andrew Thomson of Somerton, Pa., 2, waits to have his baseball signed by the Phillies' first baseman at the opening of the Pete Rose Police Athletic League Fund. Rose was manager of the Cincinnati Reds from 1984 until 1989. Rose played with the Phillies from 1979 to 1983. He helped to take the Phillies into the World Series in 1980. Phillies won the series 4 games to 2 against Kansas City.

PUBLISHED THURSDAY, NOVEMBER 27, 1980

Phillies third baseman Mike Schmidt was a highly decorated ballplayer in 1980: first in home runs, first in his league in runs batted in, and with a Gold Glove and a citation as most valuable player in the World Series to his credit. But Schmidt's earlier honors were topped when he was named, by unanimous decision, most valuable player in the National League in 1980.
UPDATE: On Monday, January 9, 1995, the esteemed Mr. Michael J. Schmidt made baseball history one last time. He was elected to the Baseball Hall of Fame with the most votes (444) received by any player in the 59 years in which the Baseball Writers Association of America has been conducting the balloting. "I guess this is kind of the topping, the icing on the cake, the culmination of a career," said Schmidt, during his half-hour news conference at Veterans Stadium, where he spent 18 seasons. Schmidt was also named most valuable player in 1981 and 1986.

PUBLISHED THURSDAY, JUNE 26, 1986

Phillies president Bill Giles, overcome by emotion, said the decision to release Carlton was his toughest as the Phils' president. The 14 ½ year Phillies career of Steve Carlton, a four-time Cy Young Award winner and certain Hall of Famer, ended Wednesday, June 26. Club president Bill Giles announced that the 41-year-old left-handed pitcher had been given his unconditional release, after Carlton rejected suggestions that he retire.

PUBLISHED THURSDAY, JUNE 26, 1986

PUBLISHED FRIDAY, JULY 28, 1978

PUBLISHED TUESDAY, SEPTEMBER 29, 1981

At bat with readers is Phillies pitcher Tug McGraw, who holds 3-week-old Candi Lees during an autographing session at Encore Books. McGraw, signing his work "Lumpy, A Baseball Fable," readily acquiesced when Candi's mother, Sissie, thrust her into his arms.

UPDATE: Frank Edwin 'Tug' McGraw, Phillies relief pitcher who fired that final fastball past Kansas City Royals outfielder Willie Wilson to wrap up the only world championship in the club's history in 1980, announced his retirement February 14, 1985.

"Waiter! There seems to be a Phillie Phanatic in my soup." Well, even if there was, no one at the Rusty Scupper in the New Market seemed to mind. Phillie Phanatic, David Raymond, stalked the restaurant handing out leaflets advertising the American Society's soccer and jogging marathon.

99

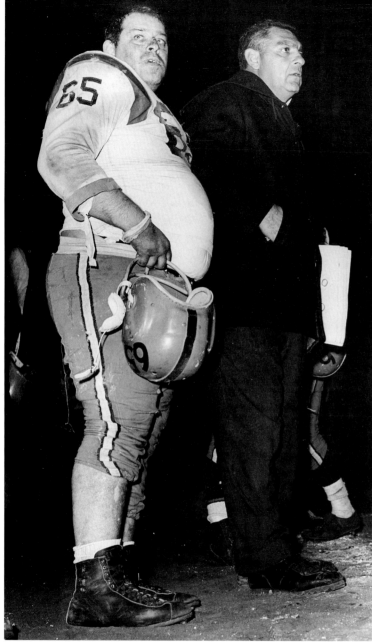

PUBLISHED SUNDAY, NOVEMBER 8, 1964

Mario DeMore (65), of New Jersey's Hammonton Bakers, is a warrior in the rough, tough world of semi-pro football, a school of hard knocks that offers no glory. Coach Joe Papiano is a bit worried over a fumble that lost their team the ball during a game with the Camden Wildcats.

PUBLISHED THURSDAY, MAY 24, 1984

On The President's Team, sports figures known as the "Reagan-Bush All Stars" arrive at the Italian Market in South Philadelphia for a day of campaigning. Left to right are former Eagles end Pete Retzlaff, former Warriors forward Tom Gola, one-time middle-weight boxing champion Joey Giardello and former Eagles line backer Chuck Bednarik.

PUBLISHED SATURDAY, APRIL 6, 1968

PUBLISHED FRIDAY, JANUARY 8, 1971

Retained Eagles' coach Jerry Williams speaks while general manager Pete Retzlaff, (left) and owner Leonard Tose appear somber during a press conference. Williams had been under strong criticism from the owner after the Eagles lost games to Baltimore and Washington and looked helpless doing it. Even a 30-20 victory over Pittsburgh in the final game failed to satisfy Tose completely. Tose announced at the hastily called press conference that Williams would return to complete his final year of his three-year contract.
UPDATE: Financial problems forced Eagles owner Leonard Tose to sell the Eagles in 1985 for about $65 million to Norman Braman.

Sixers', Wilt Chamberlain, with taped wrists, wrestles rebound away from strong left arm of Boston Celtics player-coach Bill Russell in a Spectrum playoff tilt. The Celtics jarred the 76ers, 127-118, in the Series opener. The Celtics won the series 4 games to 3.
UPDATE: In his 13 seasons with the Boston Celtics, Bill Russell won the most valuable player award five times.
UPDATE: During his 14 seasons in the National Basketball Association, Wilton (Wilt) Norman Chamberlain "Wilt the Stilt" led the league in scoring seven consecutive seasons (1959-1965) and was the most valuable player four years.

PUBLISHED FRIDAY, JUNE 1, 1979

PUBLISHED WEDNESDAY, SEPTEMBER 23, 1987

Philadelphia Eagles owner Norman Braman, with president Harry Gamble (left), answers questions on the strike. Norman Braman made two things clear. First, that the NFL owners would not cave in on the issue of free agency, and second, that the NFL players' strike had all the signs of being a long, frustrating siege. "If we gave the players the right to select the team they desired to play for, the balance we have created over the years in making football the No. 1 sport in the United States would absolutely be jeopardized," Braman said at a news conference at Veterans Stadium.

UPDATE: The 24-day-old National Football League players strike collapsed Thursday, October 15, 1987 when the union sent its players back to work without a contract.

UPDATE: Miami car dealer Norman Braman, 61, who bought the franchise in 1985 from former owner Leonard Tose for $65 million, agreed Wednesday, April 6, 1994 to sell the Eagles to Hollywood producer Jeffrey Lurie, 42, for a record $185 million.

In an emotional news conference, Bernie Parent, goalie for the Philadelphia Flyers, announces his retirement. An injury February 17 jeopardized the vision in the right eye, and he reluctantly decided to call it quits after 11 years with the team.

PUBLISHED WEDNESDAY, AUGUST 4, 1982

It was a tough fight, but a stubborn Rocky Balboa is stretched out on his back and lashed to a flatbed truck. The 2,000 pound, 8-foot, 6-inch statue, a gift from actor Sylvester Stallone who used it in the filming of the movie "Rockie III," had resisted for almost two days the most strenuous efforts to move it from its mount in front of the Philadelphia Museum of Art. Now it is down and awaiting placement on a pedestal at the Spectrum.

PUBLISHED MONDAY, NOVEMBER 29, 1971

JFK Stadium: The Morning After the Day Before. An empty jug of sherry, a wind-blown umbrella and the monumental clutter of Saturday's Army-Navy game will face a huge clean-up crew. Those in the crowd of 97,047 who sat through a steady rain on a gloomy, cold afternoon saw one of the most exciting finishes as Army held off Navy in a 24-23 thriller.
UPDATE: John F. Kennedy Stadium was demolished in May, 1992. The stadium for years was host to Army-Navy football games, historic boxing matches, Billy Graham crusades and countless concerts, including Live Aid.

PUBLISHED SUNDAY, JUNE 27, 1971

Marty Liquori relaxes in the locker room after a victory at Franklin Field. Villanova's super-miler has won every major American Championship and medal available in his running class, not just once but in some cases two and three years running. He has never lost a race in pressure-drenched Madison Square Garden (through 13 contests), and he has gone undefeated as anchor man in 10 races at Franklin Field in Philadelphia.

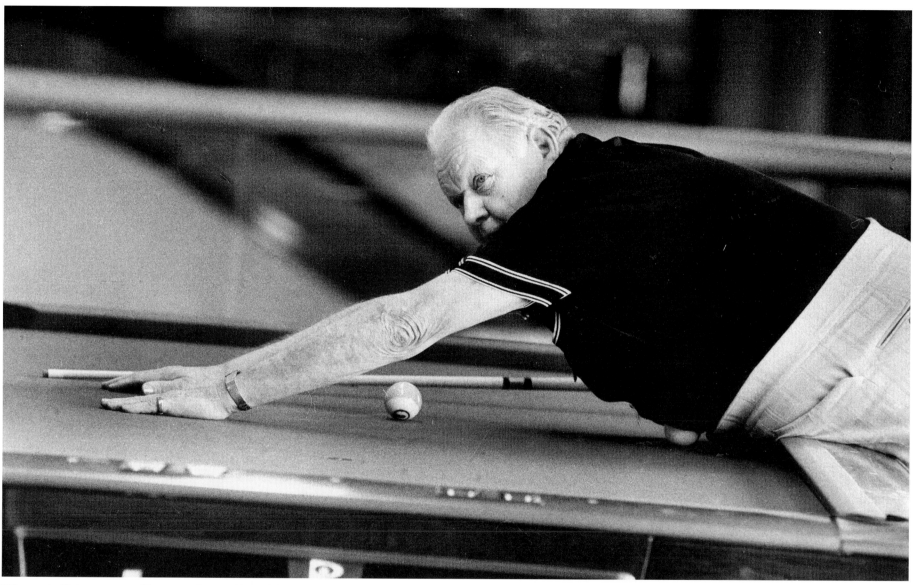

Minnesota Fats pauses to line up a shot at Harrah's Marina Hotel Casino in Atlantic City, N.J., where contestants, Willie Mosconi, Irving "Dacon" Crane, Luther "Wimpy" Lessiter, Arthur "Babe" Cranfield, Joe "Meatman" Balsis, "Cowboy" Jimmy Moore and U.J. Puckett gathered for the "Legendary Pocket Billiards Stars Tournament," a three-day elimination tournament with a grand prize of $10,000 to the winner. Fats, immortalized by the movie 'The Hustler,' was born in New York City with the name Rudolph Walderone Jr., said he first started playing pool when he was 3 ½.
UPDATE: Minnesota Fats, the pool shark who blustered his way out of smoky barrooms to become the most famous player ever to pick up a cue stick, died Thursday, January 18, 1996.

PUBLISHED WEDNESDAY, MAY 8, 1984

Crew members of the U.S. Rowing Association skim over the Schuylkill in their dragon boat in preparation for the Dragon Boat Festival International Races to be held June 10 in Hong Kong. All the members of the crew, 20 paddlers, the drummer and the stern steerer, are residents of the Philadelphia area. The Schuylkill is the group's principal training site; but, in the week before departure, workouts will be held on the Delaware River at Penn's Landing, where the "wave patterns" are similar to those in Hong Kong Harbor, site of the races.

UPDATE: Despite finishing almost 15 seconds faster than last year, a group of Philadelphians was third behind two Chinese teams June 10, 1984.

PUBLISHED TUESDAY, MAY 19, 1987

Barbara A. Smith (left) blows bubbles as Barbara Byrne Sgro watches. Both received bachelor's degrees from Wharton. The occasion at Franklin Field was the 231st time the University of Pennsylvania's officers and scholars, teachers, students and friends had gathered together to honor their best and to grant their degrees.

PUBLISHED SUNDAY, MAY 26, 1974

Grant MacAvoy of Philadelphia, a music major, became the first male to graduate from Beaver college since 1907, in commencement ceremonies at the 121-year-old Glenside, Pa., campus.

PUBLISHED THURSDAY, OCTOBER 29, 1987

At the campus of Girard College in North Philadelphia, newly installed President Don P. Sheldon has charge of a high-spirited group of children. Sheldon was chosen to head the 139-year-old prep school, which has seen major changes in recent decades. The school was built by Stephen Girard, the 19th Century banker and merchant. Upon his death in 1831, Girard left the bulk of his $7.5 million estate to the city to establish "a permanent college in which poor, white, male orphans would be housed and educated." The school is steeped in tradition, and some changes have come slowly. Lawsuits led to the admission of black male students in 1968 and to the arrival of the first girls in 1984.

Six young women registered for classes at Central High School under a court order, ending a 147-year-old all-male tradition at the city's most prestigious public high school. As the girls (from left) Jessica Bonn, Michele Hangley, Rachel Gafni, Karen Seif, Elizabeth Newberg and Pauline King began arriving about 8 a.m. and walked through the green front doors of the school, they were greeted with stares and murmurs from some of the male students, and a Welcome To Central High School entrance floor mat.

School board president Richardson Dilworth, seated 2nd from right, said the 12 city banks holding loans against the district have agreed to the district's using $7 million to meet its June 4 payroll, enabling the public schools to resume classes. They will be in session for the remainder of the school year until June 24. Also meeting with city bankers, (from left), Mrs. Lawrence Boonin, board member; Dr. Mark R. Shedd, Superintendent of Public Schools and John R. Bunting, president of First Pennsylvania Bank. Board members standing (from left), William Ross; George Hutt; Rev. Dr. Henry Nichols and Dr. Alec Washco Jr.
UPDATE: Richardson Dilworth, 75, one of Philadelphia's liveliest, most respected and most controversial public figures died January 23, 1974. State and local officials praised former Mayor Richardson Dilworth as "one of Philadelphia's greatest citizens" who pioneered sweeping reforms in city politics and government.

110

PUBLISHED TUESDAY, NOVEMBER 3, 1987

Teacher Josephine Bevilacqua Piccirillo listens to an answer at Spruance Elementary School in Northeast Philadelphia. An informal effort by a teacher to teach one student Italian has, since late September, mushroomed into more than 31 children clamoring for Italian instruction and giving up their recess to get it. "I think they're trying to tell us something," said the teacher, delighted by the turnout in a school that has no foreign language program. Piccirillo, a fourth-grade teacher and a native of Italy, is amazed by their response.

PUBLISHED FRIDAY, MAY 6, 1966

Narcotics victims speak out during a joint state legislative committee probing the use of drugs in high schools and on college campuses. Howard Quinley, special investigator for the joint state legislative committee probing use of drugs, adjusts mask for John, who told how addiction to a succession of drugs ruined his college career.

PUBLISHED TUESDAY, MAY 19, 1969

Former Vice President Hubert H. Humphrey signs autographs for high school students at the Bellevue Stratford where he addressed the Citizens Committee on Public Education. Students are (from left) Fred Smith, Simon Gratz; Cheryl Green, Gillespie Jr. High; Candy Feiner, Girls High; and Bernie Brandt, Northeast High. Humphrey came to town to urge voter approval of the $90 million school bond issue on Tuesday's primary ballot. UPDATE: Philadelphia voters defeated the $90 million school construction loan proposal May 20, 1969, but approved the loan question in the November election.

PUBLISHED SATURDAY, MAY 24, 1975

Wearing black arm bands in a sixth-grade classroom at St. Denis School in Havertown, Pa., children and their teacher, Sister Dorothy Anne, show a form of mourning over a U.S. Supreme Court decision against state aid to parochial schools. The flag was lowered to half-mast at Catholic schools throughout the state because of the ruling.

PUBLISHED WEDNESDAY, NOVEMBER 14, 1984

St. Casimir Parochial School pupils Melissa Lemba, 11, and John Drumstas, 12, display poster for essay contest with stop-smoking theme "I Love You - Please Stop Smoking." Albert Einstein Medical Center, Mount Sinai-Daroff Division, announced an essay contest open to all pupils, grades five through twelve, in public and parochial schools in the area served by the center. John Drumstas, a seventh-grade pupil at St. Casimir in South Philadelphia, had seen the mother of a friend die of lung cancer at the age of 28, and it troubled him. "They said she got cancer from smoking. I didn't like to hear that, because my mother smokes."

PUBLISHED WEDNESDAY, MARCH 19 1986

PUBLISHED THURSDAY, APRIL 21, 1977

For three years sixth-grade students at the Highland Park School in Upper Darby, have had a healthy respect for the firefly. They have gained statewide, even national attention, for their efforts in getting a law enacted designating the firefly as the state insect. Act 59 was signed on April 10, 1974, by Pennsylvania Governor Milton J. Shapp. A handsome bronze plaque, held by principal William Bambrick was presented to the school by community groups in honor of the 26 students.

At William Dick Elementary School, high tech and Mother Nature have come together to teach pupils a lesson in biology. Pupils (from left) Raheim Brittingham, Kevin Davis, Latasha Williams and Rashan Coles examine a newborn chick. Using a video camera and a TV monitor, kindergarten and elementary pupils are able to watch incubated eggs hatch into chicks. The chicks will be used in life science classes at the school.

PUBLISHED TUESDAY, AUGUST 27, 1985

In a meeting of Northern Ireland and West Philadelphia, Sister Falaka Fattah, co-director of the city's House of Umoja, walks with Irish youths who are visiting as part of an international exchange program to address problems of street violence. In turn, five residents of the House of Umoja, a center for delinquent youths, visited Northern Ireland for four weeks. The House of Umoja was chosen for the project, part of the President's International Youth Exchange, conducted by the U.S. Information Agency, because of the considerable amount of work it has done with international visitors on behalf of the U.S. government.

PUBLISHED SATURDAY, JULY 5, 1975

The Fourth of July was celebrated in a variety of fashions in the Philadelphia area. For William White of North Philadelphia, it was a great day in South Philadelphia's League Island Park where he barbecues the spareribs for his family.

PUBLISHED SATURDAY, JULY 5, 1975

Joe McGurn (left) and Bob Millet (on ladder) prepare flag display on South 18th Street as part of the Fourth of July celebration, 199 years after it all began and at the place it began, Independence Hall, Philadelphia.

PUBLISHED SATURDAY, APRIL 26, 1975

Independence Hall is a shrine for all seasons. Rain or shine, this venerable structure where American Independence was born nearly two centuries ago always holds its attraction. The lore of Independence Hall and the Liberty Bell holds something for everyone, from school children on class trips to senior citizens. As they walk through the building, they examine the Liberty Bell, visit the Assembly Room in the East Wing, where the Declaration of Independence was adopted, and inspect the Long Gallery (or Long Room, as it was known at the time the Founding Fathers were inventing a nation) on the second floor. At one minute past midnight on July 4, 1976, the bell was moved from Independence Hall to the Liberty Bell Pavilion where it now rests on display. The Liberty Bell Pavilion, built for the Bicentennial, sits opposite Independence Hall on Independence Mall between Chestnut and Market Streets.

PUBLISHED WEDNESDAY, APRIL 17, 1985

Awaiting the thud of the wrecker's ball, Benny Krass says a prayer across the street at Krass Bros. Men's Store, 937 South Street. Benny Krass had been tempted to stay home and avoid the pain of watching the wrecker's ball strike the building, a piece of South Street history, where his family's clothing store opened 38 years ago. But he finally decided that he ought to be there because "it wouldn't be fair not to say goodbye." The Krass Bros. Building that Benny has made famous as the "Store of the Stars" was being razed by the Philadelphia Redevelopment Authority to make way for a shopping plaza.

PUBLISHED FRIDAY, AUGUST 29, 1986

At 87, founder of Termini Bros. Bakery, Joseph Termini, sprinkles powdered sugar on fresh cream puffs and cannoli at his bakery on South Eight Street. "I will retire," he says "when I die." Termini is the surviving founder of the Termini Bros. Bakery, one of the best-known establishments of its kind in Philadelphia.
UPDATE: Termini, 95, died Wednesday, December 21, 1994.

PUBLISHED SATURDAY, MARCH 5, 1988

The real McCoy is what's being held by three granddaughters of Maria Nacchio, the founder of Philadelphia's famed Federal Pretzel Co., 636-38 Federal Street in South Philadelphia. Established in 1922, the soft pretzel bakery is now owned and operated by the granddaughters, all of whom shifted from other careers to take charge of the company. They are (from left) Norma Nacchio Conley, 52, Florence Nacchio Sciambi, 54, and Gloria Nacchio Alter, 49. "Our grandmother couldn't have known, of course, when she started the business, that the three of us would be running it some day," Conley said, "But I think she would have been pleased."

PUBLISHED WEDNESDAY, APRIL 27, 1977

A smiling Philadelphia Mayor Frank L. Rizzo returns to his City Hall office after being named "honorary Paramount Chief of the Zahn Clan" of Liberia. Dr. Melvin J. Chisum, who visited Liberia recently and was himself made a clan chief, presented the robe and hat to the mayor on behalf of clan chief Jimmy Dahn, who met Rizzo when he was here last year.

PUBLISHED THURSDAY, APRIL 10, 1980

Joe Stock, construction superintendent for J. Gross Construction, stands amid rubble inside Whitemarsh Hall in Wyndmoor, Pa. In its prime, it was one of the most opulent mansions, which cost financier Edward T. Stotesbury nearly $3 million to build six decades ago and $1 million a year to maintain. It was a country home built for his second wife, Eva.

119

PUBLISHED MONDAY, OCTOBER 31, 1977

High atop a roof in Lititz, Pa., William Geiger watches his assistant, Thomas Reimer, clean a chimney. The outfits are old-fashioned, but the technique is up-to-date. Like a throwback to Charles Dickens's London, the burly chimney sweep wears the uniform that really puts him in the 19th Century: black top hat, black wool sweater and pants, and over it all, a black coat with tails. William Geiger, when he is not a chimney sweep, is a teacher of industrial arts education at Millersville State College in Lancaster, Pa. Geiger did considerable research into past practices before deciding on his 19th Century garb, which he maintains, "I honestly don't wear for advertising."

PUBLISHED SATURDAY, JUNE 30, 1984

Rigger Bill Van Horn secures a rope for moving Reading Terminal's 92-year-old clock. The clock still attached to a six-foot stem, hung for a moment like a gray Victorian lollipop over the sidewalk at the corner of 12th and Market Streets outside Reading Terminal in Philadelphia. The four-faced Reading Terminal street clock, its hands stopped at 10 minutes to 1, its four dials faded or shattered, was taken down and trucked away for a much needed restoration.

PUBLISHED FRIDAY, NOVEMBER 14, 1970

PUBLISHED TUESDAY, OCTOBER 13, 1981

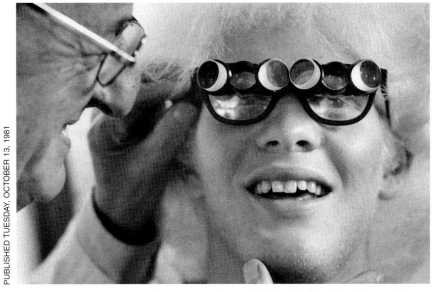

Dr. William Feinbloom, who creates glasses for legally blind patients, adjusts the six lenses on Raymond Braco's glasses which allow the legally blind Haverford College freshman to see clearly. Braco, 17, is the 150th patient to be fitted with the special glasses, and the Philadelphia College of Optometry is showing him off because the glasses he is wearing have been considerably refined since they were developed 2½ years ago. The glasses are called "honeybee lenses" because they are based on the principal that endows bees and other insects with wide peripheral vision.

Being caught with egg on your face is a good idea now and then; that is, if it is an egg facial. This is but one of the effective home beauty treatments that housewives can do themselves for mere pennies by using foodstuffs from the refrigerator or pantry. Here's a sample you can try out at home with ingredients found right in your own kitchen. For the egg on your face mask (to tighten the skin): Beat two egg whites until they are stiff. You can use them alone or mix in a little talcum powder. Apply the mixture over the face, avoiding the eye area. Leave on about 15 minutes. You'll feel it tighten. On the eye area, it is suggested you apply castor oil during the egg facial, topped off with a slice of cucumber over each eye. It is soothing.

Up for adoption, both the Boeing 707 and Atlas missile will become sights of the past when the Franklin Institute expands its Science Park. The Franklin Institute is seeking someone who will take a real, full-size jet plane off its hands. The cost: Free. The catch: You have to pay moving expenses, which could total $250,000. The 1960 aircraft has been seen by an estimated six million visitors since it opened to the public in April 1976.

UPDATE: In April, 1988, the missile was taken back to its manufacturer. The 707 was sold for the sum of $100,000 to a Memphis, Tenn., firm that deals in airplane spare parts.

Steps leading from one street to another are common in the hills of Manayunk, located in the Northwest section of Philadelphia. A youngster makes his way down the steps from Terrace Street to Tower Street overlooking a community in economic transformation, where unique attractions draw visitors, writers and artists from afar. Manayunk, a "melting pot" of races and cultures, took its name from the Indian "Manaiung" (where we go to drink). In 1983, the Manayunk Canal and Main Street were named to the National Historic Registry.

For the late great dame of Philadelphia's Broad Street, more than 35,000 items—everything from the Hunt Room's marble-topped bar to hundreds of bathroom scales—went on sale as the Bellevue Stratford's redevelopers seek to turn the hotel's contents into cash before converting the landmark building into an office, retail and hotel complex. Among the Bellevue's 35,000 items is a mountain of pillows on the ballroom stage. Diane Ghavis tops off the pile.

PUBLISHED FRIDAY, JUNE 18, 1982

Cadets stand on the mast yards of the Simon Bolivar as the ship approaches Penn's Landing with its sails furled. On parade and passing in review were 31 tall ships making their way to this port that has been here on the Delaware for 300 years.

PUBLISHED TUESDAY, OCTOBER 12, 1976

In the best Viking tradition, a ship from Essington, Delaware County, sails by the Benjamin Franklin Bridge on its way to attempt to upstage Columbus Day at Penn's Landing, where a copy of Columbus's ship Santa Maria was berthed.

PUBLISHED THURSDAY, FEBRUARY 24, 1983

Doctors at the Hospital of the University of Pennsylvania announced the first two pregnancies in women who participated in the medical center's 'in vitro' fertilization program. Dr. Richard W. Tureck, coordinator of HUP's program, displays two eggs in the fertilization process.

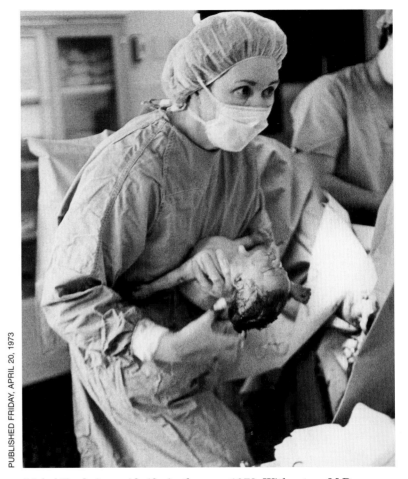

PUBLISHED FRIDAY, APRIL 20, 1973

Mabel Forde is a midwife, in the year 1973. Without an M.D. degree, she delivers several babies a week. Forde delivers babies at Booth Maternity Center, a Salvation Army Facility in Overbrook. Booth is the only Philadelphia Hospital where nurse-midwives outnumber doctors six to two.

UPDATE: Maternity and Family Activities, a nonprofit organization that has operated the Booth Maternity Center in Overbrook, formally purchased the facility Tuesday, September, 16, 1986, from the Salvation Army, now renamed the John B. Franklin Maternity Hospital and Family Center.

UPDATE: The Franklin Maternity Hospital closed its doors January 28, 1989 and was later acquired by St. Joseph's University.

PUBLISHED WEDNESDAY, OCTOBER 24, 1973

Canada geese fly in formation toward the Schuylkill River near the Strawberry Mansion Bridge in Philadelphia, after foraging on the west bank of the river.

PUBLISHED TUESDAY, OCTOBER 6, 1987

Dermatologist Albert M. Kligman's acne research led to his wrinkle discovery Retin-A, an acne drug that also appears to be effective in treating wrinkles and undoing some of the damage of age. Dr. Kligman and his colleagues found that applying tretinoin, the key ingredient in Retin-A, could partially reverse or prevent many of the changes associated with aging skin. Tretinoin, also known as retinoic acid, is a chemical derivative of vitamin A.

PUBLISHED WEDNESDAY, JUNE 6, 1984

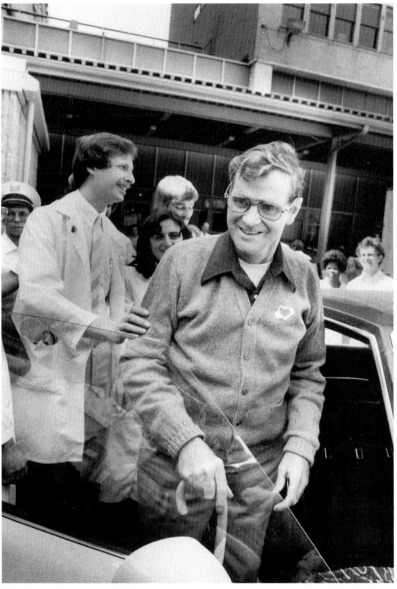

Six weeks ago, Randall Duvall could barely breathe. With a new heart beating in his chest, Duvall rose from his hospital wheelchair, walked 20 feet to his car and, with his wife in the driver's seat, headed home. Walking with the aid of a cane, his departure from Temple University's Health Sciences Center came six weeks to the day after the heart of a 16-year-old gunshot victim was implanted in his chest, making him Philadelphia's first heart transplant patient.
UPDATE: Randall Duvall, 50, died September 21, 1984. The death of Duvall, a resident of Chester Springs, Chester County, was attributed to kidney failure and pneumonia.

PUBLISHED WEDNESDAY, NOVEMBER 6, 1985

Grasping the brush in his teeth, Jules Epstein is completing a watercolor of the Parkway in Center City. He is a quadriplegic who paints a picture by holding brushes in his mouth to apply the paint. Epstein, 56, has been disabled since he was injured in a diving accident when he was 28. Still a rookie as a painter, he's one of 80 professional disabled artists from throughout the world whose work is displayed in the Sixth International Exhibition of Artists with Physical Disabilities going on in Philadelphia, sponsored by Moss Rehabilitation Hospital.

PUBLISHED SATURDAY, AUGUST 8, 1970

Bessie Smith, 42, whose incredible renditions of the blues still echo through the annals of music in the ears and voices of living artists, lay in Mount Lawn Cemetery in Sharon Hill for 33 years with only blades of grass to mark the spot. The Philadelphia Inquirer Action Line arranged for money for the tombstone to be donated—half and half—by blues-rock singer Janis Joplin and Juanita Green, a registered nurse who met Bessie at the old Lincoln Theater at Broad and Lombard Streets in the 1930's. Her career skyrocketed in the 20's when she reportedly was earning $2,500 a week and recording such songs as "Gimme a Pigfoot," "Nobody Knows You" and "Money Blues." An admirer kneels before the new grave marker.
UPDATE: Blues singer Bessie Smith, 42, was inducted into the National Women's Hall of Fame July 15, 1944. "The Empress of the Blues" made 160 recordings with jazz greats like Louis Armstrong and Benny Goodman. She died in 1937.

Stuart Gootnick adjusts a miniature candle in his reproduction of the Touro Synagogue of Newport, R.I., the oldest extant synagogue building in the United States. It is known in history as the home of the congregation to which President George Washington in 1790 wrote his classic declaration of religious liberty. Gootnick, 56, was at the National Museum of American Jewish History at Independence Hall East installing the model for exhibition.

PUBLISHED THURSDAY, APRIL 17, 1986

PUBLISHED SATURDAY, MAY 31, 1986

Cecil Gates (standing) and Skip Crabtree tie the scale model of the battleship Arizona to a pier at Penn's Landing in Philadelphia. The Arizona was sunk during the bombing of Pearl Harbor in 1941 and still serves as a tomb for 1,102 of her crew members. The miniature ship (34-foot—20:1 scale—working model) was built and is owned by Cecil Gates and his wife, Pat, retired schoolteachers from California. The model is calling here en route to New York, where it will participate in the Independence Day celebration of the 100th birthday/restoration of the Statue of Liberty.

PUBLISHED THURSDAY, NOVEMBER 17, 1977

Valerie Chiccino draws a stare while parking a miniature gasoline-powered Corvette near the specialty store at the Ardmore Shopping Center, in Ardmore, Pa. The Corvette, only $695, from FAO Schwartz, will hit 15 m.p.h., and is something special for the children on Christmas.

PUBLISHED THURSDAY, MAY 9, 1968

Mules plod the well-worn towpath beside the Delaware Canal, pulling a barge full of tourists through the New Hope, Pa. Scenic Area as their ancestors once pulled freight. In the last few years, in the square mile that makes up this artists' community, you can find history, modern art, and ancient sculpture. With more than one million visitors a year, the town is booming as a shopping mecca and a nightlife spot.

PUBLISHED SUNDAY, OCTOBER 28, 1973

Free wash job, compliments of Philadelphia, proves to Kevin Marelo the old adage about municipal services showing up when least expected. Marelo was under his car adjusting the shift mechanism when the street washers turned up on 5th Street near Chestnut, bringing Marelo up for air in a hurry.

130

PUBLISHED FRIDAY, OCTOEER 22, 1976

City Councilman John B. Kelly Jr. (left) gestures in mock triumph as he approaches the platform inside City Hall Courtyard where Thacher Longstreth, president of the Greater Philadelphia Chamber of Commerce, waits and wins the Great Train-Auto Chase by 65 seconds. The Great Train-Auto Chase began at the Port Kennedy railroad station, on the Reading division's Pottstown line.

UPDATE: John B. "Jack" Kelly Jr., 57, Philadelphia sportsman, Olympic medalist and member of one of the city's most beloved families, died March 2, 1985, after he collapsed while jogging in Center City.

PUBLISHED SATURDAY, AUGUST 31, 1974

PUBLISHED FRIDAY, APRIL 25, 1980

South Philadelphia's Marconi Day celebration brought the area's senior citizens to Marconi Plaza, Broad Street and Oregon Avenue, including 92-year-old Joseph Candelori who views the festivities with less than enthusiasm. But for most of the crowd, it was an afternoon of dancing, eating and watching the entertainment provided annually by the Marconi Senior Citizens Club.

Jim and Hazel O'Connor listen downstairs for footsteps in the attic of Carpenters Hall where they get the ghostly feeling that the First Continental Congress may still be going on. The O'Connors are the resident custodians-curators of Carpenters' Hall, in Philadelphia where the First Continental Congress convened. And periodically, they say, they are awakened in the middle of the night by sounds of vigorous debate emanating from the room in which the Congress met on the first floor.

PUBLISHED SATURDAY, MARCH 19, 1977

On the Schuylkill River, in Philadelphia, a sculler rows under the Pennsylvania Railroad Bridge in the mist.

133

PUBLISHED THURSDAY, SEPTEMBER 25, 1980

PUBLISHED SATURDAY, FEBRUARY 15, 1986

Frank Talent, of Municipal Court, experiences the Seatbelt Convincer while holding a 35-pound sack of sand, which represents a baby, against his chest. The Convincer descended when put into gear, only to be brought to an abrupt stop. Philadelphia Mayor W. Wilson Goode, experiencing the Convincer, announced that all drivers and occupants of city vehicles would be required to wear seat belts. The Seatbelt Convincer, a PennDot Machine, simulates a low-speed accident.

For those who turn out at John F. Kennedy Stadium, there will be a double thrill: The thrill of seeing stunts and the thrill of providing scholarships for the children of police officers and firefighters who have died in the line of duty. Those who will participate in the 26th annual Hero Scholarship Fund Thrill Show held a dress rehearsal. Patrolman Chick Kurtz, on his motorcycle, defies the law of gravity driving down a stand platform.

PUBLISHED THURSDAY, AUGUST 29, 1968

Highland Fling is demonstrated by James Liddell, 78, a member of the Scottish Historic and Research Society, in "Salute to Scotland" show at PMC College (1972, renamed Widener University) in Chester, Pa.

PUBLISHED TUESDAY, OCTOBER 31, 1978

Getting a little advice, Philadelphia Mayor Frank L. Rizzo listens to Mrs. Sondina Fortucci, 88, during a courtesy call; she had recently been ill. The mayor had just come from a ground-breaking across the street at Passyunk Avenue and Dickenson Street, the old Moyamensing Prison site, which will be the site of an Older Adult Center.

135

PUBLISHED TUESDAY, MAY 20, 1969

Chief William Red Fox, nephew of Chief Crazy Horse who figured in the defeat of General George Custer at Little Big Horn in 1876, does a War Dance with Miss Elaine Mitnick. Chief Red Fox, 99, in full Indian regalia, was greeted at City Hall, where he presented an Indian headdress to Philadelphia Mayor James H.J. Tate. Chief Red Fox, of the Ogalala Sioux Tribe, says he can still remember the battle of the Little Bighorn River, even though he was only six. Concerning General Custer he was most uncomplimentary, not only because he lacked military skill but because Custer was a "rat."
UPDATE: William Red Fox, 105, died March 1, 1976 in Corpus Christi, Texas.

PUBLISHED TUESDAY, NOVEMBER 16, 1976

Promoting love, singer-composer Stevie Wonder visited Wills Eye Hospital in Philadelphia. "Steve Wonder's the greatest," said Darrell Cooke, 7, of Sharon Hill, Pa., an outpatient in the hospital's Fight for Sight Clinic. "He can sing better than anybody in this whole world."

PUBLISHED SATURDAY, OCTOBER 5, 1974

Members of the cross-country teams at Archbishop Ryan and Overbrook High Schools, took advantage of a beautiful day for practice runs on Belmont Plateau in Fairmount Park. Philadelphia's multi-faceted skyline has changed considerably in the last five years.

PUBLISHED THURSDAY, AUGUST 21, 1969

Volunteers preparing for the Philadelphia Folk Festival wear garb likely to be in abundance at this weekend's show at Old Pool Farm, near Schwenksville, Pa., site of the 8th annual Philadelphia folk fete.

PUBLISHED SATURDAY, FEBRUARY 22, 1975

Spring-like weather brought this couple out for climbing and sunning at the Logan Circle fountain in Fairmount Park. The couple, Stuart Shills, 20, of Philadelphia, and Janis Gluck, 20, of Ventura, Calif., took advantage of a sunny day and temperatures in the 50s for their outing.

138

PUBLISHED MONDAY, MARCH 29, 1976

Patrick O'Brien, 10, takes advantage of a spring breeze to launch his fancy kite, the Phoenix and the Snake, from the steps of the Philadelphia Museum of Art overlooking the Benjamin Franklin Parkway and City Hall.

PUBLISHED THURSDAY, OCTOBER 19, 1984

Officer Clarence Deveaux, with his family and relatives, after he was cited for his heroism. Forty-five of Philadelphia's "finest" were honored at City Hall for bravery, valor and heroism. The heroism awards were "for an act of heroism and outstanding courage without regard to personal safety, which results in the saving of a life."

PUBLISHED SATURDAY, JULY 3, 1982

Instructor Robert Heisman with graduates Debbie Anastasi (left) and Cynthia Bernier, who were among 140 men and women, after months of training, became members of the Philadelphia Police Department. The recruits, Class 258, received diplomas from Mayor William J. Green during a graduation ceremony at the Civic Center. They will go on duty right away.

PUBLISHED SATURDAY, SEPTEMBER 29, 1984

Some of 52 graduates of the Police Academy listen during the ceremony at the Port of History Museum where Mayor W. Wilson Goode urged Philadelphia's new police officers to resist temptations to trade their new badges for money and asked them to commit themselves to improving the tainted image of the Philadelphia Police Department. The mayor said that "there is no finer police department in this country than the one we have here," but that it had been tainted by "a few who have drifted away."

PUBLISHED TUESDAY, JUNE 14, 1983

A youth seeks shelter from the swelter with a flamboyant swan dive into the fountain at the Philadelphia Museum of Art. The area was cooking from blasts of heat, sultry air and temperatures in the 90s, and no rain in sight.

142

PUBLISHED FRIDAY, APRIL 10, 1987

After toying with the hearts of Philadelphians for the last few weeks, spring is forecast to make another glorious appearance, bringing light breezes and a high of about 70. Trying to put his surroundings to canvas, Jonathan Greenberg of Germantown stood amid flowering cherry blossoms near the Girard Avenue Bridge on Kelly Drive. Greenberg, 30, a former social worker who has been painting for about five years, says he is hoping to make it his new career.

PUBLISHED THURSDAY, MARCH 29, 1984

It was the ninth day of spring. And yes, it was less than two weeks away from the Phillies' home opener. But the weather in and around Philadelphia was not very spring-like to a pedestrian struggling to overcome gusting winds and rain at 15th and Market Streets.

PUBLISHED THURSDAY, OCTOBER 25, 1984

MIRROR, MIRROR, on the walk, whose reflection is tallest of all? In Center City, the shimmering winner and still champ is City Hall Tower, as seen from a courtyard puddle rippling from drizzle droplets and pedestrian footsteps. The view was one of the few saving graces of the damp autumn chill in Philadelphia.

144

PUBLISHED FRIDAY, SEPTEMBER 2, 1977

Strapped to a padded dolly, Theresa McNulty, 6, takes mobility therapy at the United Cerebral Palsy Association of Philadelphia and Vicinity. Theresa is one of 500 clients who are being served by the agency, which covers Bucks, Chester, Montgomery and Philadelphia counties. The program includes services for infants, preschoolers and severely handicapped adults, vocational training, sheltered workshops, employment opportunities, social service and recreational activities.

PUBLISHED TUESDAY, AUGUST 25, 1987

Helen Claudia DeGennaro, 2, indicates to her grandmother Helen DeGennaro, 84, a terminally ill cancer patient, that she would soon be 3 years old. "Welcome to my home," says Helen DeGennaro with formal hospitality to those who visit her sick-bed, set up in the living room of the Germantown house she has lived in for 30 years. DeGennaro is able to do so thanks to the Wissahickon Hospice, a health-care agency based in Chestnut Hill that helps people die at home with as much dignity and as little pain as possible.

PUBLISHED TUESDAY APRIL 1, 1980

Dr. Harold G. Scheie, 71, founding director of Philadelphia's Scheie Eye Institute, is seen after performing an operation in the $12 million facility named after him.

UPDATE: Dr. Scheie, 80, an internationallly known ophthalmologist who saved the sight of thousands of patients while operating at his Scheie Eye Institute in West Philadelphia, died March 5, 1990. Dr. Scheie was a legendary surgeon who identified a rare eye disease that was named after him. He also was widely known for developing surgical techniques to treat cataracts and glaucoma. Dr. Scheie had a habit of not charging poor patients.

PUBLISHED SUNDAY MAY 1, 1983

Poet Nicholas Virgilio, 55, at his home in Camden, N.J., writes haiku poetry. It is his job, his career, and his hobby, the thing he loves most in the world. Haiku, the Japanese art of writing poetry in 17 syllables (according to purists), is often used as an introduction to poetry for children in American schools.

UPDATE: Virgilio, 60, died January 3, 1989 while taping a segment of the CBS-TV program Nightwatch. His book, *Selected Haiku*, a collection of 20 years' work, was first published in 1985. His most famous poem appeared in 1987 on the cover of the *New York Times Book Review* as an example from a newly published collection of American haiku.

PUBLISHED MONDAY, MARCH 21, 1988

Dr. Carl L. Tinkelman, a Cherry Hill, N.J. root-canal specialist, checks the teeth of Xavira the rhino at the Philadelphia Zoo. He's been volunteering as a zoo dentist for 12 years now. The root-canal specialist says he would devote his working hours to what he has been doing on a volunteer basis since 1976; "hanging out" at the zoo.

147

PUBLISHED TUESDAY, MARCH 1, 1988

A polar bear's idea of fun is a zookeeper's bid for better animal mental health. While Klondike splashes with a pair of plastic balls, curators at the Philadelphia Zoo are working on ways to liven up the animals' lives. "We are trying to add more spice to their lives," said Karl Kranz, curator of mammals at the 42-acre zoo, who is considered a leader in the national effort to improve the stimulation of zoo animals. "It's really occupational therapy for the animals." One of the playthings that tigers and bears have enjoyed most is the "boomer ball," a large, heavy-duty polyethylene ball made in Grayslake, Ill.

PUBLISHED SUNDAY, JULY 6, 1980

The dallying llama creates his own traffic jam at Great Adventure, which is divided into two discrete sections, the amusement park and the safari. The 450-acre park is stocked with 2,000 wild animals, all of whom seem to have nothing better to do than camp out on the road or just a few yards from it.

PUBLISHED SUNDAY, MAY 6, 1973

"Ma Mu," a 65 pound golden gibbon ape from Thailand is owned by Jeanne Lefkowitz of Laurel Lane Farm in Newtown, Bucks County. "Ma Mu," also a "watch ape," hugs her pet cat. She doesn't like strangers and will sound off with a shrill in short blasts...like an air raid siren.

148

PUBLISHED THURSDAY, FEBRUARY 2, 1978

Hold that tiger, you might have fervently hoped had you been involved in this, ah, delicate operation at the Philadelphia Zoo. But Monty, a four-year-old Siberian tiger, all 300 pounds of him, underwent a root-canal operation, and was a "very cooperative" patient of Dr. Carl L. Tinkelman, a Cherry Hill, N.J. root-canal specialist. The dental surgery was a success.

PUBLISHED WEDNESDAY, NOVEMBER 30, 1977

Ordinary house cats have made Yuri Koklachov the clown prince of the Moscow Circus. Through an interpreter, Yuri says it fills his heart with joy to make people laugh. It has always been that way with him. Yuri does what no other clown in Russia can do and something few people in the world can do. He performs with trained domestic cats.

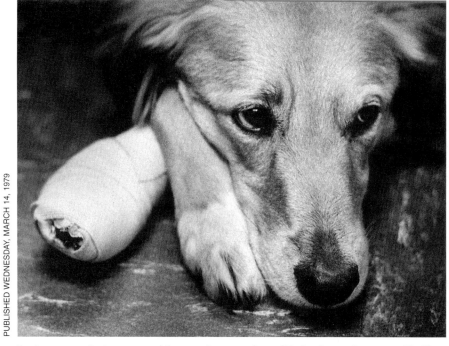

PUBLISHED WEDNESDAY, MARCH 14, 1979

Lady, a cross between a golden retriever and a collie is about six years old. She vanished after leaving her home and owners, Sidney and Rena Benjamin, in the Philadelphia Wynnefield section, to romp with other dogs on the nearby Bala Cynwyd Golf Club course. Lady was later found in Fairmount Park, her left paw caught in a steel leghold trap. The paw was so badly infected that surgeons at the Hospital of the School of Veterinary Medicine of the University of Pennsylvania, determined that the entire leg should be removed. Mrs. Benjamin was asked, What will it be like to have a three legged dog? "Who's counting legs?" Benjamin said. "Lady's back, and that's all that matters."

PUBLISHED SATURDAY, NOVEMBER 8, 1975

Tuff, rrrrrruff stuff—if canines can look indignant, Caesar does so in reaction to the audacity of a 5-week-old pup doing a dance of acquaintanceship at the JFK Plaza. As Patrolman James Martinez of the Police Canine Corps and his shepherd watch, their companion shepherd Caesar gets the business from Little Bit, a miniature shepherd whose owner, Sabu Elaine Gonzalos of Philadelphia, says Little Bit has no fear.

PUBLISHED WEDNESDAY, AUGUST 14, 1985

Kibee Jones is greeted by his dog, See-See. Jones, who lives in South Philadelphia, is a junkman. He says he's headed for his 113th birthday. He said he was born December 15, 1872, on a plantation near St. George, S.C., to parents who had been slaves only seven years earlier. Both parents died when he was an infant, and he was raised by his maternal grandparents.

SUNDAY, JANUARY 12, 1969

Gypsy Rose Lee made her first in-person appearance in Philadelphia. "I have visited friends here many times," Miss Lee told reporters at the Sheraton. "But I never played Philadelphia." She sat down at the table to put on a pair of high-heeled golden slippers. "Hey Gypsy," somebody said, "you're supposed to be taking it off, not putting it on." Miss Lee is vice president of the company that makes Voila dog food.

PUBLISHED MONDAY, MAY 17, 1965

Michael Viola, a *Philadelphia Inquirer* photographer, started to paint his third floor three weeks ago, but a family of robins had other plans. They built a nest on a window sill. Viola put away his paint brushes. It was worth the delay. A parent feeds one of the five fledglings.

PUBLISHED SUNDAY, AUGUST 4, 1968

Robespierre, a toy poodle owned by Peter Waxman of Philadelphia, rests atop an auto while taking a 15-minute look at the sights at Independence Hall.

PUBLISHED FRIDAY, JULY 27, 1973

The world turned upside down for this baby kangaroo when he tried a fast exit from his mother's pouch at the Philadelphia Zoo.

PUBLISHED SATURDAY, AUGUST 17, 1974

Kensington children race along the 2200 block of E. Williams Street, which was closed to traffic for a playstreet and a fund-raising festival Friday. The playstreet, in Philadelphia, is one of five kept open to children in the Kensington area through the cooperation of the United Neighbors of Kensington and the Urban Coalition, who have been working to end racial tension among young people.

155

PUBLISHED TUESDAY, OCTOBER 30, 1984

It's a struggle, but Anne Fenhagen, 2 ½, crawls along the climbing stiles at the Chestnut House Child Care Center in the Mid City YWCA in Philadelphia. Physical fitness, coupled with childhood learning, comes early to youngsters in the "Kindergym" program. Children at the day-care center, infants and toddlers included, spend part of the sessions in a special program of hands-on experiences.

PUBLISHED TUESDAY, JUNE 15, 1971

Kindergarten pupils at St. Peter's School, 319 Lombard Street, Philadelphia, display the colors on Monday during ceremonies in observance of Flag Day.

PUBLISHED FRIDAY, OCTOBER 2, 1981

PUBLISHED WEDNESDAY, AUGUST 6, 1986

The expression, "It's as American as apple pie," reflects the deeply held and fundamentally correct notion that there is something right about apples. Not only are apples good to eat, they're fun to pick, too. At the Nussex Farms in West Chester, Pa., little picker Danielle Cugino, 3, of West Chester, had her arms full of apples and eyes on more.

At the Kohl family farm in Bucks County, Tina Gehan, 2, of Pineville, Bucks County, milks a cow. Her family is hosting a Fresh Air Fund Child from Brooklyn, N.Y. The New York-based, nonprofit agency has provided free summer vacations to 1.7 million low-income New York City children since its 1877 inception. Last year, more than 10,000 children, from ages 6 to 16, visited 327 towns in 13 states and Canada. So far this year, 125 Fresh Air boys and girls have stayed in Montgomery and Bucks Counties.

PUBLISHED WEDNESDAY, SEPTEMBER 7, 1983

The Labor Day weekend was a hot and hazy one in the Philadelphia area, as the mists shrouding the Society Hill Towers and the U.S. Customs House, at right, show. But the hot weather did not stop Edwin Concepcion, 15, from riding his bicycle in Wiggins Waterfront Park, in Camden, N.J.

PUBLISHED SUNDAY, MARCH 29, 1964

With mule in tow at Collingswood High School gym, Diane Hall lunges for a loose ball during a "donkey basketball" game in Collingswood, New Jersey. Proceeds from the game aid the school's student exchange program.

PUBLISHED SATURDAY, APRIL 26, 1975

During a class trip to Independence Hall, students are in awe as they gaze upon the 2,000 pound Liberty Bell, cracked during the ringing to celebrate George Washington's birth, after repairs were made to the bell for the third time in 1846. After that ringing, the bell was silenced forever. In 1839, anti-slavery activists adopted the bell as a symbol of freedom and the title "Liberty Bell" was attached. The title stuck and the bell became a national icon.

PUBLISHED SUNDAY, JUNE 23, 1968

Form is everything as demonstrated by Richard Hicks, 11, who does a back dive at the city's newest swimming pool at the Kendrick Recreation Center in the Roxborough section of Philadelphia.

PUBLISHED MONDAY, JANUARY 24, 1966

The first sledding of the season brings youngsters to the slopes behind the Art Museum while wet snow swirls around them, painting a pretty wintry scene that partially makes up for the hazardous conditions the storm created.

PUBLISHED MONDAY, JUNE 20, 1977

John Nepoumcene Neumann, the "Little Bishop of Philadelphia," was entered into the Calendar of the Saints, Sunday, June 19, before tens of thousands of pilgrims from all over the world, gathered in St. Peter's Square in what Pope Paul VI called an atmosphere of "festive joy." It was 10 a.m. in Vatican City and the resonant bells of St. Peter's Basilica were tolling the hour when Pope Paul recited in Latin the formula of canonization, and when it was over the silence was broken by applause. A statue of Pius IX, who was Pope during John Neumann's eight years as Bishop of Philadelphia, overlooks the pilgrims who came to celebrate the canonization in St. Peter's Square.

PUBLISHED MONDAY, JUNE 20, 1977

Nuns attending the canonization enjoyed snapping pictures for the folks at home.

PUBLISHED MONDAY, JUNE 20, 1977

A woman is in awe as she looks at a tapestry of St. John Neumann at St. Peter's Basilica.

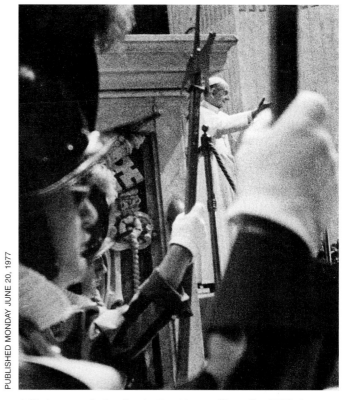

PUBLISHED MONDAY JUNE 20, 1977

A Swiss guard stands at attention as Pope Paul VI gives his blessings to pilgrims attending services at St. Peter's Basilica after the canonization of John Neumann.

PUBLISHED MONDAY, JUNE 20, 1977

Presenting a canonization gift of two ruffed grouse, the Pennsylvania state bird, Larry Mueller of Darby, Pa., kneels before Pope Paul VI.

PUBLISHED FRIDAY, AUGUST 6, 1976

Leaders of the Roman Catholic, Episcopal and Lutheran churches in America joined in predicting the end of the "lovers quarrel" that has separated the Christian churches since the 16th Century. The "ecumenical program" of the International Eucharistic Congress was marked by expression of unity, conciliation and openness to change. An Indian dances before papal legate James Cardinal Knox on Independence Mall in Philadelphia.

PUBLISHED FRIDAY, FEBRUARY 12, 1988

In a splendid ceremony descended from Medieval coronations, Anthony Joseph Bevilacqua was installed as the seventh archbishop and eleventh bishop of the Catholic Archdiocese of Philadelphia. Archbishop Bevilacqua, 64, (left), accepted the symbolic staff of authority from Cardinal John Kroll with expression of humility and humor, and with a clear call for the Philadelphia area's 1.35 million Catholics to "drive out demons of all kinds," from poverty and homelessness to pornography and abortion.

UPDATE: Cardinal John Kroll, 85, died Sunday, March 3, 1996 at his home in Overbrook. He was an unshakable pillar of tradition and authority during an era of tumultuous change in the Roman Catholic Church.

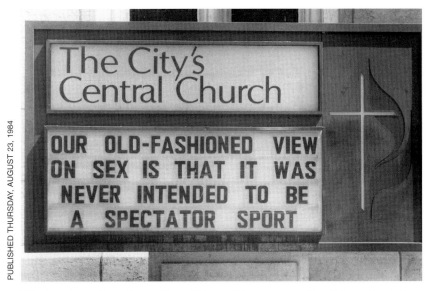

PUBLISHED THURSDAY, AUGUST 23, 1984

What we have here is another of those "Sermons on the Sidewalk" at the Arch Street United Methodist Church, Broad and Arch Streets in Philadelphia. Pedestrians passed the message board on the Broad Street side of the building, and at least half of them did a double take.

PUBLISHED SATURDAY, APRIL 10, 1982

As other demonstrators follow, Tim Ahrens, coordinator of American Christians for the Abolition of Torture, carries a six-foot wooden cross along the Parkway past the Cathedral Basilica of SS. Peter and Paul. The march, held in protest of Latin American governments that practice torture, was one of several processions and prayer services held in the Philadelphia area in commemoration of Good Friday.

PUBLISHED SATURDAY, JULY 21, 1984

The Rev. Wycliffe Jangdharrie, pastor of the Reformed Seventh-Day Adventist Church in Germantown, is seized by park rangers Gary Hartley (left) and Bobby Spears at Independence Hall after he refused to identify himself to federal park rangers who tried to serve him with citations for demonstrating without a permit and passing out leaflets without a permit. He was protesting the jailing of the Rev. Sun Myung Moon.

PUBLISHED FRIDAY, AUGUST 6, 1976

Mother Teresa, arriving at Independence Mall for the Mass for Native Americans during the Eucharistic celebration. About 4,000 people turned out for the special Mass celebrated by the Rev. John Hascall, a Franciscan priest who is a Chippewa Indian. The service incorporated songs and gestures from a number of American Indian tribal traditions.
UPDATE: Mother Teresa, nun, patron of the poor and Nobel laureate died of heart failure Friday, September 5, 1997, at the order she founded in Calcutta 50 years ago. She was 87.

PUBLISHED THURSDAY, MAY 31, 1979

Archbishop Chrysostomos of Cyprus greets parishioners in St. George Cathedral of the Greek Orthodox Church in Philadelphia after officiating at a Divine Liturgy. Archbishop Chrysostomos delivered a forceful and moving sermon about the plight of his beloved homeland, that strife-torn island nation in the Mediterranean that was partially occupied by Turkey in 1974. When the archbishop said that Cypriots "would never rest until all of Cyprus is liberated," there went up a great cry.

MONDAY, JULY 29, 1974

Ignoring threats of discipline, words of protest and pledges by their bishop not to let them practice, 11 women deacons were ordained Episcopal priests. The new priests had begun their newly conferred duties, and offered Communion for those who knelt at the altar rail after the ordination. (From left) the Rev. Carter Heyward, of New York; the Rev. Katrina Sivanson, of West Missouri; the Rev. Merrill Bittner of New York; the Rev. Marie Moorefield of New York and the Rev. Alla Bozarth-Campbell of Minnesota. The Episcopal Church has condemned the ceremony, saying that it violates church law.